NEW Roadhouse
RECIPES

From the Editors of The MILEPOST.

More memorable recipes from roadhouses, lodges, bed and breakfasts, cafés, restaurants and campgrounds along the highways and byways of Alaska and Canada.

Morris Communications Company LLC

⊰ New Roadhouse Recipes ⊱

Photography: All photos courtesy of the recipe contributors or MILEPOST® staff.

Cover Photos: Sheep Mountain Lodge entrance © David L. Ranta, staff. Insets from top–¹Spamadillas © Fly By Night Club; ²Sheep Mountain Lodge interior © David L. Ranta, staff; ³Smoked Salmon Spread © David L. Ranta, staff; ⁴© 7 Gables Inn.

Recipes were solicited from the contributors. Recipes were reviewed by editors and in some cases, tested, but the publisher offers no guarantee of individual results.

Editors: Carol A. Phillips and Leah R. Burke
Managing Editor: Kris Valencia Graef
Design/Production: David L. Ranta
Fulfillment Director: Gail Weaverling
Fulfillment Manager: Fran Jarriel
Manufacturing Director: Kevin Miller
General Manager: David C. Foster
Publisher: William S. Morris III

Publisher of: Alaska Roadhouse Recipes, The MILEPOST®, The Alaska Wilderness Guide, Alaska A to Z, The MILEPOST® Souvenir Logbook, Alaska Magazine.

ISBN 1-892154-13-7
Key title: New Roadhouse Recipes
Printed in U.S.A.

Morris Communications Company LLC
735 Broad Street, Augusta, Georgia 30901
www.morris.com

MORRIS
COMMUNICATIONS
COMPANY•LLC

Editorial Offices:
301 Arctic Slope Avenue, Suite 300
Anchorage, Alaska 99518
Phone (907) 272-6070 • Fax (907) 275-2117
www.themilepost.com

Contents

Contents

Introduction

© Glacier Bay Country Inn

New Roadhouse Recipes takes you on a culinary road trip through the North, visiting old-time roadhouses and modern lodges, inns, hotels, bed and breakfasts and cafés, along the highways and byways featured in our All-The-North Travel Guide®, The MILEPOST®. The dishes served along the way are re-created in this cookbook. We invite you to try these recipes in your own kitchen, or drop in on our contributors and let them prepare the dish for you.

The recipes are grouped according to highway or destination, reflecting the order of highways and destinations in The MILEPOST® travel guide. The recipes are also arranged in geographical order. In other words, they appear according to the location of the contributor on the highway, in the same order as they would appear on a drive North.

The first thing any traveler will notice on a trip North is that the farther north you drive, the fewer the conveniences along the way (until you reach a major population center). For all the years that have passed since the Alaska Highway opened up this region to public travel in 1948, it is still largely an unsettled wilderness. And while roadside businesses don't face the shortages of materials so common in the early days along the highway, they still often have to make do with what's available locally. So you may see salmon and local berries on the menu, rather than kiwi and coquille St. Jacques (although many of our Northern chefs bring with them a tradition of more exotic fare).

For anyone running a highway business in the North, it also means doing a half-dozen other jobs in addition to planning the day's menu and preparing the food. As one of our highway hosts remarked, you don't have to worry about waking him up too early in the summer because he doesn't sleep until the end of August anyway.

Our thanks to the many contributors who shared their house specialties with us so that we could share them with you. Our roadside chefs are as varied as their recipes, but all share one thing in common: A desire to please their guests with a home-cooked meal. And therein lies the secret of Northern cuisine.

West Access Route

The West Access Route is the most direct route for West Coast motorists to the start of the Alaska Highway at Dawson Creek, BC. Beginning in Seattle, WA, this route heads north through British Columbia's rugged Fraser River Canyon to Prince George. From there, the West Access Route follows the Hart Highway, crossing the Rocky Mountains at Pine Pass before descending into the rolling farmland surrounding the community of Dawson Creek.

The following recipes are from the kitchen of Judy Vernon, who acted as food consultant on the first Alaska Roadhouse Recipes book published by Geoff Vernon, her husband and greatest fan.

An accomplished cook, Judy frequently entertained Geoff's staff–including The MILEPOST® field editors–at the Vernons' home in Bellevue, Washington, where great food and gracious hospitality were the standard fare. Judy and Geoff were killed in a plane crash in Mexico in September 2001. These recipes were chosen by their son Trevor Vernon, who remembers them as some of his mom's best "comfort" foods. These recipes–and this book–are dedicated to the memory of Geoff and Judy Vernon.

CHICKEN, ARTICHOKE AND PARMESAN BAKED PENNE

Judy Vernon
Bellevue, WA

4 Tbs. **butter or margarine**

2 Tbs. **olive oil**

1 lb. **boneless, skinless chicken breast, cut into 1" pieces**

1 1/4 tsp. **salt**

1/4 tsp. **black pepper**

2 cups **cremini mushrooms, sliced**

2 Tbs. **minced garlic**

1 Tbs. **fresh thyme, chopped**

1 tsp. **dry oregano**

1/8 tsp. **cayenne pepper**

6 Tbs. **flour**

5 cups **milk**

1 lb. **dry penne pasta**

1/2 cup **kalamata olives, chopped**

1 can (13.75 oz.) **artichoke hearts, drained and coarsely chopped**

1/3 cup **green onions, sliced**

1 cup (3.5 oz.) **high-quality Parmesan cheese, grated and divided**

2 cups (7.5 oz.) **Mozzarella cheese, grated**

Preheat oven to 375°F.

In a large saucepan, heat butter and olive oil over medium-high heat. Add chicken pieces and season with salt and pepper. Sauté for about 3 minutes or until chicken turns opaque. Add sliced mushrooms and cook for 2 minutes or until limp. Add garlic, thyme, oregano and cayenne and stir for about 20 seconds. Do not let garlic brown. Stir in flour and cook for about 1 minute, stirring constantly. Immediately add milk, stirring vigorously with a whisk. Bring to a simmer and whisk occasionally until sauce is thickened, about 6 to 7 minutes. Remove from heat, and set aside.

Bring a large pot of water to a boil and cook penne pasta until done, according to package directions. Drain.

In a large bowl, mix together pasta and sauce. Then, fold in kalamata olives, artichoke hearts, green onions, 3/4 cup Parmesan and Mozzarella cheeses until well-combined. Place mixture into lightly buttered or pan-sprayed 9" X 13" baking pan. Sprinkle top with remaining 1/4 cup Parmesan and bake for 25 to 30 minutes or until pasta is heated through, sides are slightly bubbling and top is golden brown.

Serves 6 to 8.

HOT CHICKEN SALAD

Judy Vernon
Bellevue, WA

2 cups **chicken, cooked (boiled) and diced**
2 cups **celery, thinly sliced**
1 package **chopped almonds**
1 tsp. **pimiento, cut up**
1 cup **mayonnaise**
2 Tbs. **lemon juice**
2 Tbs. **onion juice**
3/4 cup **crushed potato chips**
1/2 cup **American cheese, grated**

Mix together chicken, celery, almonds and pimiento. Mix mayonnaise, lemon and onion juices and pour over chicken mixture. Put mixture in shallow casserole dish (9" X 13" pan). Fill a bag with potato chips and cheese. Pound and shake bag until chips are crushed and cheese is mixed together with chips. Pour over top of chicken mixture and bake at 350°F for 15 to 20 minutes.

Serves 4.

MANICOTTI

Judy Vernon
Bellevue, WA

$1/2$ lb. **ground beef**
1 **clove garlic**
1 cup **cream-style cottage cheese**
4 oz. **shredded Mozzarella cheese**
$1/2$ tsp. **salt**
$1/2$ cup **mayonnaise**
8 **manicotti, uncooked**
1 16-oz. jar **spaghetti sauce**
$1/2$ tsp. **dried oregano leaves**
Parmesan cheese to garnish

Brown meat and garlic in skillet. Drain fat. Blend cottage cheese, Mozzarella cheese, salt and mayonnaise in a bowl. Stir in meat. Fill each manicotti with $1/4$ cup filling. Place in baking dish. Sprinkle with remaining filling and cover with sauce. Sprinkle with oregano and Parmesan and cover with foil. Bake at 325°F for 15 minutes. Remove foil and bake for 10 minutes.

Serves 6 to 8.

NUTS & BOLTS

Judy Vernon
Bellevue, WA

$^1/_3$ cup **margarine**
1 Tbs. plus 1 tsp. **Worcestershire sauce**
$^1/_2$ tsp. **salt**
$^1/_8$ tsp. **garlic salt**
1 cup **Cheerios® cereal**
1 cup **Rice Chex® cereal**
1 cup **Wheat Chex® cereal**
1 cup **thin pretzels**
1 cup **peanuts**

Melt margarine in shallow pan. Stir in Worcestershire sauce, salt and garlic salt. Add cereal, pretzels and peanuts and stir gently. Heat in 300°F oven for about 30 minutes, stirring gently every 10 minutes.

Serves 8 to 12.

STEAK DIANE

Judy Vernon
Bellevue, WA

6 **beef filets, 1" thick**
2 to 4 Tbs. **butter**
2 oz. **brandy**

Sauce:
2 Tbs. **butter**
6 **shallots, thinly sliced**
6 **mushrooms, thinly sliced**
4 Tbs. **chives or 2 green onion tops**
2 Tbs. **parsley**
2 Tbs. **Worcestershire sauce**
salt and pepper

For sauce: Sauté mushrooms and shallots in butter. Add remaining sauce ingredients.

Pound filets until 1/2" thick. Sauté over high heat in foaming butter. Turn after 2 1/2 minutes. Put a little sauce on top of each filet. Continue cooking steaks over high heat for 2 minutes. Pour brandy into pan, and flame. Serve immediately.

Serves 6.

SALMON BURGERS

Debbie McKinney
Salmon House Restaurant
Hell's Gate Airtram
Mile A 83.6 Trans-Canada Highway 1 East

5 lbs. **coho salmon (grated while frozen)**
1 cup **bread crumbs**
1/2 cup **liquid egg**
1/2 **green pepper**
1/2 **red pepper**
1/2 **white onion**
1/2 **green onion**
1/4 **head celery**
1/4 tsp. **garlic powder**
1/4 tsp. **black pepper**
1/4 tsp. **seasoned salt**

Mix all ingredients together well. Shape into patties. Cook until inner core temperature reaches 165°F for 15 seconds or longer.

To store uncooked patties, layer individual patties between waxed sheets sprayed with non-stick cooking spray, and freeze. Defrost in fridge.

Yields 10 to 15 patties.

East Access Route

A High Rigg Retreat B&B

The East Access Route was the only overland route to Dawson Creek, BC, when the Alaska Highway opened to civilian traffic in 1948. The East Access Route begins in Great Falls, MT, then heads north through central Alberta and two of the province's 2 largest cities, Calgary and Edmonton. From the provincial capital of Edmonton, the East Access Route connects with the Alaska Highway at Dawson Creek, BC, via either Highway 43–passing through the canola fields between Valleyview and Grande Prairie–or Highway 2, the historic drive from Athabasca past Lesser Slave Lake.

FARM CAKES

Delton and Phil Gray
A High Rigg Retreat B&B
Mile J 11.9 Devonian Way Bypass

"Afternoon tea is served to guests upon arrival, and these two recipes are always a hit."

3 cups **flour**
2 cups **granulated sugar**
2 tsp. **baking soda**
1/2 cup **cocoa**
2 cups **water**
2/3 cup **oil**
2 Tbs. **vinegar**
2 tsp. **vanilla**

Filling:
8 oz. **cream cheese, room temperature**
1/3 cup **granulated sugar**
1 **fresh egg**
pinch **of salt**
6 oz. **semi-sweet chocolate chips**

Preheat oven to 350°F. Prepare 18 muffin cups. Sift together flour, sugar, baking soda and cocoa. Add water, oil, vinegar and vanilla. Beat at medium speed for 3 minutes until well combined.

For filling: In another bowl, cream the cream cheese. Add sugar, egg and salt and beat until smooth. Fold in chocolate chips.

Pour chocolate batter into muffin cups and spoon a teaspoon of filling into the center of each cake. Bake for 20 to 25 minutes or until cake springs back when lightly touched. Enjoy!

Yields 18 cakes.

"A lovely country home with superb views of the North Saskatchewan River valley, the house is named after a family home in the Lake District, England. High Rigg means 'high on the hill' in Cumbrian, which is a fitting description for both High Riggs.

"The original High Rigg was constructed on the first piece of land to be donated to the National Trust in 1917. The Canadian High Rigg does not share the same history, being built in the 1960s, but was one of the first homes built in the rolling countryside between Edmonton and Devon. Later, the original owner subdivided for agricultural and residential development.

"Guests will enjoy the rustic comforts and special touches of this unique B&B as well as the abundance of wildlife in the area. Close proximity to the International Airport, Edmonton, Devon, Spruce Grove, and Stony Plain makes this a convenient location for travelers.

"High Rigg is adjacent to the new Black Hawk golf course, 5 miles east of the Devonian Botanic Garden, and just 15 minutes from West Edmonton Mall."

LEMON BREAD
Delton and Phil Gray
A High Rigg Retreat B&B
Mile J 11.9 Devonian Way Bypass

1/2 cup **shortening**
1 cup **granulated sugar**
2 **fresh eggs**
1 **lemon rind**
1/2 cup **milk**
1 1/2 cups **bread flour**
1 tsp. **baking powder**
pinch **of salt**

Frosting:
1/4 cup **granulated sugar**
juice of 1 lemon

Mix all bread ingredients in mixer. Pour into a loaf pan and bake at 350°F for about 55 minutes, until done. (Test with a toothpick.)

For frosting: Combine sugar and lemon juice. Spoon over loaf while still hot.

Yields 1 frosted loaf.

Alaska Highway

Midnight Sun
Bed & Breakfast

Kluane
Bed & Breakfast

Coal River Lodge & RV

Mae's Kitchen

Shepherd's Inn Ltd.

Kidd's B&B

Built by military and civilian engineers in 1942, the Alaska Highway was and is a truly remarkable achievement: More than a thousand miles of road through a vast expanse of Northern wilderness. Although today's Alaska Highway has been paved, rerouted here and there, and offers many more services than the original pioneer road, it remains a great adventure for motorists.

The Alaska Highway begins at Mile 0 in Dawson Creek, traveling northwest across the Rocky Mountains in northern British Columbia. The Alaska Highway crosses into the Yukon at Watson Lake, then winds west to the territorial capital of Whitehorse before continuing on to the international border at Port Alcan. The official end of the Alaska Highway is 200 miles from the border at Delta Junction, AK, Historical Mile 1422.

BASIC PANCAKE
David Kidd
Kidd's B&B
Dawson Creek, BC

(Recipe comes from 1960s Edmunds Cookbook from New Zealand.)
"We serve this recipe with a fresh fruit puree and/or syrup.
"This is a simple recipe which is popular with many people. I use whole wheat or a blend of white and whole wheat flour. I add fruit, either slices of bananas, apples, strawberries or blueberries as available."

1 **egg**
$1/4$ cup **vegetable oil**
1 tsp. **vanilla**
2 cups **flour**
$1/4$ cup **granulated sugar**
1 tsp. **salt**
4 tsp. **baking powder**

Beat egg, oil and vanilla. Add flour, sugar, salt and baking powder, and beat until smooth. Add milk if needed to achieve desired consistency.

Add fruit such as apples, bananas or berries to batter if desired. Cook pancakes on hot, oiled griddle for about 2 to 3 minutes on each side, or until done.

Serve with fresh fruit puree or syrup if desired.

Serves about 6.

SMOKY BARBEQUE SAUCE

Teresa Erb
The Shepherd's Inn Ltd.
Historic Mile 72 Alaska Highway, BC

2 Tbs. margarine
$1/4$ cup onion, chopped
$1/2$ cup brown sugar
$1/2$ tsp. salt
$1/2$ tsp. garlic powder
$1/2$ tsp. dry mustard
$1/8$ tsp. cayenne pepper
1 tsp. vinegar
1 tsp. Worcestershire sauce
1 tsp. liquid smoke
1 cup ketchup

Melt margarine in a heavy saucepan. Add onion and brown sugar. Combine dry spices and add to the saucepan.

Combine vinegar, Worcestershire sauce and liquid smoke and stir into sauce. Add ketchup and heat to boiling over low heat, stirring often. Remove from heat and serve.

Yields 2 cups.

DATE CAKE
Elizabeth Raja
Mae's Kitchen
Historic Mile 147 Alaska Highway, BC

1 lb. **dates**
1 tsp. **baking soda**
1 cup **boiling water**
1/2 cup **soft margarine**
1 cup **granulated sugar**
2 **eggs**
1 1/2 cups **flour**
1 tsp. **baking powder**
1/2 tsp. **salt**
1 tsp. **vanilla**

Topping:
3 Tbs. **margarine, melted**
1/2 cup **brown sugar**
4 to 5 Tbs. **milk**
1 cup **coconut**

Soak dates and baking soda in boiling water and set aside. Cream margarine, sugar and eggs. Combine flour, baking powder and salt. Alternating the date mixture and the dry ingredients, add to creamed mixture and mix well. Mix in vanilla. Pour batter into a 9" X 9" pan and bake at 350°F for 35 to 40 minutes.

For topping: Mix all topping ingredients together well and spread evenly over top of cake. Broil at 350°F until golden brown.

Serves about 15.

CHOCOLATE FUDGE COOKIES

Donna Rogers
Coal River Lodge & RV
Historic Mile 533 Alaska Highway, BC

1 cup **margarine or butter**
1 1/2 cups **granulated sugar**
2 **eggs**
2 tsp. **vanilla**
2/3 cup **cocoa**
3/4 tsp. **baking soda**
1/2 tsp. **salt**
2 cups **flour**
1 1/2 cups **chocolate chips**

Cream butter, sugar, eggs and vanilla. Blend dry ingredients, add to creamed mixture and mix well. Fold in chocolate chips. Drop by teaspoonful, 1" apart, onto lightly greased cookie sheet. Flatten slightly. Bake at 350°F for 10 to 12 minutes.

Yields 3 dozen.

SPECIAL TOMATO OMELET

Farshid and Del Amirtabar
Midnight Sun Bed & Breakfast
Whitehorse, YT

2 Tbs. **olive or cooking oil**
2 cups **chopped tomato**
salt and black pepper to taste
8 **eggs, well-beaten**
1/2 cup **cheddar cheese grated**
1 tsp. **dry coriander or cilantro**

Heat oil in medium-sized frying pan. Add tomato and fry until well-cooked and slightly browned. Add salt and pepper and mix well. Add eggs on top, but do not mix. Sprinkle cheese then dry herbs over top. Cover and cook on medium heat for 10 to 15 minutes or until cooked.

Serves 4.

BEET JELLY

Cecile M. Sias
Kluane Bed & Breakfast
Historic Mile 1053 Alaska Highway, YT

3 cups **beet juice**
1 box **Certo® crystals**
2 Tbs. **lemon juice**
4 cups **granulated sugar**
1 box **cherry JELL-O® brand gelatin**

Boil beet juice with Certo. Add sugar, lemon juice and
JELL-O® powder. Bring to a hard boil, then pour into jars.

Yields about 4 to 6 8-oz. jars.

RHUBARB SPREAD

Cecile M. Sias
Kluane Bed & Breakfast
Historic Mile 1053 Alaska Highway, YT

"This spread is excellent on hot cakes, French toast or regular toast."

6 cups **rhubarb, cut into pieces**
1 1/2 cups **granulated sugar**
1/2 cup **water**
1 package **strawberry JELL-O® brand gelatin**

Boil rhubarb with sugar and water until stewed. While hot, mix in JELL-O®. Applesauce can be substituted for JELL-O®.

Serves 24.

Yellowhead Highway

The Yellowhead Highway is a trans-Canada highway that connects with access routes to the Alaska Highway at Edmonton, Alberta, and at Prince George, British Columbia. The Yellowhead Highway ends in Prince Rupert, BC, port for Alaska state ferries and B.C. Ferries plying the Inside Passage.

WARM WILD MUSHROOM SALAD

Guy Brouillette, Executive Chef
Overlander Mountain Lodge
Mile E 182.4 Yellowhead Highway

Executive chef Guy Brouillette of the Overlander Mountain Lodge has an advantage. To make his mushroom salad, he just goes for a hike around the lodge, located at the eastern edge of Jasper National Park, and picks his own. He starts with morels in early June and finishes up with oyster and lobster mushrooms at the end of the summer. The rest of us will just have to be content with what we can find at the grocery store.

Lettuce mix:
2 cups **spring mix lettuce leaves**
fresh thyme, basil and tarragon for garnish
2 **tomatoes, cut into 8 wedges**
1 **yellow pepper, julienned with seeds removed**

Mushrooms and dressing:
Approximately 3 cups **mixed mushrooms: oyster, morel and button**
1 **medium onion, very finely chopped**
1 tsp. **fresh thyme, minced**
1 tsp. **fresh tarragon, minced**
1 tsp. **rosemary, minced**
1 tsp. **sage, minced**
fresh ground pepper
sea salt to taste
1/4 cup **balsamic vinegar**
1/4 cup **red wine vinegar**
lemon juice to taste
1/2 cup **extra virgin olive oil**

Arrange lettuces, herbs, tomatoes and yellow peppers on 4 plates. Sauté the mushrooms, onions and herbs in a little oil for approximately 2 minutes in a hot frying pan. Whisk vinegars, lemon juice and oil together to make dressing. Combine and place on salad mix.

This salad is a terrific accompaniment to grilled chicken or trout. This dish is also delicious served cold. To transport, pack lettuces separately from tomatoes, peppers and mushrooms. Cook and dress the mushrooms and place in a securely lidded container. Assemble just before serving.

Serves 4.

OVERLANDER CHEESE CAKE

Terry Lewis, Chef
Overlander Mountain Lodge
Mile E 182.4 Yellowhead Highway

Base:
1 1/4 cups **graham cracker crumbs**
3/4 cup **almonds, ground**
2 oz. **butter**
1 Tbs. **granulated sugar**

Filling:
1 1/4 lbs. **cream cheese**
juice and zest of 1 lemon
7 **eggs**
1 Tbs. **vanilla**
1 1/4 cups **granulated sugar**

Mix all base ingredients, and pat down into a 10"
springform pan. Bake at 375°F for about 15 minutes, until
lightly browned.

Mix all filling ingredients and pour over baked crust. Bake
at 300°F for 2 hours. Slide a small knife around the edge of
the cake after baking to separate the cake from the pan. This
will keep your cake from cracking as it cools.

Serves 10 to 12.

PUFFY FRITTATA WITH HAM AND GREEN PEPPERS

Edna Bryanton, EJ's Roost B&B
Grande Cache, AB

"Leftovers are great. Just put frittata in a pan, and reheat in the oven for 5 to 10 minutes."

2 Tbs. **butter**
1 small **onion**, chopped
1 **green pepper**, chopped
8 slices (6 oz.) **ham**, chopped
$^1/_2$ tsp. **salt**

$^1/_2$ tsp. **ground pepper**
8 large **eggs**, at room temperature
$^1/_4$ cup **water**
$^1/_2$ cup **shredded cheddar cheese**

Preheat oven to 250°F. Melt 1 Tbs. of the butter in a 12" nonstick frying pan over low heat. Add onion, green pepper, ham, $^1/_4$ tsp. salt and $^1/_4$ tsp. of pepper. Cook, stirring occasionally. Transfer to plate.

Separate eggs, yolks in a medium bowl and whites in a large bowl. Lightly beat yolks with water and remaining salt and pepper. Beat egg whites until they form stiff (but not dry) peaks. Fold yolks into whites.

Melt remaining 1 Tbs. butter in an oven-safe pan over low heat. (I like to use a round pan.) Pour in eggs and spread evenly with a spatula. Sprinkle onion and pepper mixture evenly over eggs. Then, sprinkle ham mixture and cheese over eggs. Cover and cook until eggs are set, 25 to 30 minutes. Slide frittata onto plate and serve immediately.

Serves 4.

WHOLE GRAIN CREPES WITH BANANA AND KIWI

Edna Bryanton, EJ's Roost B&B
Grande Cache, AB

Crepes:
1 cup whole wheat pastry flour
$1/4$ tsp. salt
1 egg
1 cup plus 3 Tbs. unsweetened soy milk or whole milk
1 $1/2$ tsp. vanilla extract
2 tsp. butter
1 to 2 Tbs. water

Filling:
$1/2$ cup plain yogurt or whipped cream
1 banana, cut into 16 diagonal slices
2 kiwi fruit, peeled, cut in half lengthwise and sliced
2 tsp. lime juice (optional)
$1/2$ tsp. cinnamon

For crepes: In a large bowl, combine flour and salt. In a small bowl, beat egg, then stir in milk and vanilla. Pour into flour and mix well. Melt $1/2$ tsp. butter in an 8" nonstick frying pan over medium heat. Pour 3 Tbs. of batter into the pan and tilt the pan to coat the bottom in a thin layer. If batter seems too thick, add 1 to 2 Tbs. water. Cook first side until nicely browned, about 2 minutes. Turn the crepe and cook the second side for 2 minutes (the second side will look spotted). Slide the crepe onto a plate and cover with foil to keep warm. Repeat process with remaining batter, buttering the pan after every other crepe.

For filling: Place crepe on a serving plate, attractive side down, and spread with 1 Tbs. yogurt or cream. Add 2 banana slices and $1/4$ of the kiwi fruit in strips. Sprinkle filling with lime juice and a pinch of cinnamon, and fold or roll up crepe. Repeat with remaining crepes, putting 2 crepes on each plate.

Yields 8 6" to 7" crepes. Serves 4.

Syrup for Frozen Peaches

Jackie Johnson
Lakeside Resort
Mile PG 37.6 Yellowhead Highway

"This is a delicious topping for ice cream."

Juice of 6 small oranges
Juice of 6 small lemons
2 cups **pineapple juice**
5 cups **granulated sugar**
1 case **peaches (about 25 lbs.)**

Mix orange, lemon and pineapple juices and sugar together to make syrup. Peel and slice peaches and put them into freezer bags with enough syrup to cover. Lay bags on cookie sheet and freeze.

To serve, thaw in refrigerator, but make sure some ice crystals remain in fruit.

Yields 9 bags.

GRILLED SALMON ON BLUEBERRY BANNOCK

Adrianne Johnston
Cow Bay Café
Prince Rupert, BC

"This recipe was developed for a local TV program. I use fresh blueberries and fresh local salmon. It's a fast and easy recipe."

Bannock:
2 cups **flour**
2 tsp. **baking powder**
1 tsp. **salt**
2 Tbs. **dried blueberries**
$^1/4$ cup **Crisco® shortening, melted**
1 to 1 $^1/4$ cups **milk or water**
oil for deep frying

Mix together flour, baking powder, salt and dried blueberries. Melt Crisco and cut into flour mixture. Mix gently until incorporated. Add liquid and gently mix into dough. Heat oil in wok or large skillet or stir fry pan at 350°F. Roll dough out to $^3/4$" thick. Cut into 4" X 4" squares. Fry one at a time until done. Cool on rack.

Fresh Mango-Blueberry Salsa:
1 **fresh, perfectly ripe mango**
1 **fresh jalapeño, seeds and membranes removed**
$^1/4$ cup **tiny ripe blueberries (fresh), washed and dried**
1 Tbs. **fresh lime juice**
salt, sugar and chili powder to taste

Peel, seed and dice mango into tiny pieces, dice jalapeño into tiny pieces and mix together with blueberries. Add lime juice and seasoning and mix gently.

Salmon:
4 4-oz. **salmon filets, skinned and boned**

Season salmon as desired [Adrianne uses southwest flavoured seasoning]. Drizzle with olive oil and grill over medium heat until just done.

To serve, split bannock. Spread bottom half with mayonnaise and a fresh lettuce leaf. Top with salmon and salsa and top half of bannock.

Serves 4.

View from Cow Bay Cafe, located along the waterfront northeast of downtown Prince Rupert.

The revitalized Cow Bay area boasts numerous cafes, boutiques, a popular pub and 2 bed-and-breakfasts. The ambience is historic (antique phone booths, old-fashioned lampposts), but the theme is bovine, with businesses and buildings bearing cow names (like Cowpuccinos, a coffee house) or cow colors (black and white pattern).

Cassiar Highway

Wildflour Coffee Shop

Kathy's Korner Bed & Breakfast

Once a remote mining road to mineral resources in the Cassiar Mountains, today's Cassiar Highway has become a scenic route to the Alaska Highway for many travelers.

This 446-mile all-weather road junctions with the Yellowhead Highway at Kitwanga, BC, then heads north along the Coast Mountains and through the Cassiar Mountains to join the Alaska Highway just west of Watson Lake, YT.

SALMON LOAF
WITH SOUR CREAM CRUST

Kathy Tschakert
Kathy's Korner Bed & Breakfast
Hyder, AK

2 lbs. precooked salmon, skinned and boned
1 cup onions, chopped
1 Tbs. rosemary leaves
1 tsp. garlic powder
1 tsp. lemon pepper
2 cups crushed bread crumbs
3 eggs
1 Tbs. celery seed
cheddar cheese, sliced, to cover loaf
green and red peppers, sliced, to cover loaf

Sour Cream Batter:
1 cup **Bisquick®** mix   1/4 cup **sour cream**
1/4 cup **milk**   1 **egg**

Flake or mash cooked salmon. Add onions, rosemary, garlic powder, lemon pepper, bread crumbs, eggs and celery seed and mix well. Pat into greased loaf pan. Layer cheese slices over top to cover. Then, layer peppers over top to cover. To make batter, combine all batter ingredients together and mix well. Batter will be very sticky. Completely cover top of loaf with batter. Bake at 350°F for 25 to 30 minutes or until cooked through.

This recipe is good served with sour cream and dill sauce.

Serves 6.

ALASKA FRUIT PIE

Bonnie Barrett
Wildflour Coffee Shop
Hyder, AK

"This is our most popular pie!"

2 9" prepared pie crusts with high fluted edges

Filling:
4 cups **rhubarb, diced**
2 cups **fresh strawberries, sliced**
2 cups **fresh (or frozen, thawed) blueberries**
2 1/2 cups **granulated sugar**
6 Tbs. **cornstarch**

Crumb topping:
1 cup **granulated sugar**
1 cup **flour**
3/4 cup **butter**

Stir fruit, sugar and cornstarch together. Turn into prepared crusts. In another bowl, cut butter into flour and sugar until crumbly. Divide crumbs between pies. Bake at 425°F for about 30 minutes until edges brown. Cover lightly with foil and continue baking 10 to 15 minutes more until bubbly. Cool and serve with whipped cream or a scoop of ice cream.

Serves 12.

Wildflour Coffee Shop is located in Hyder, Alaska.

WILDFLOUR'S FAMOUS SPLIT PEA SOUP

Bonnie Barrett
Wildflour Coffee Shop
Hyder, AK

"This was a sellout every time!"

7 cups **dried split peas**
12 cups **water**
12 cups **chicken stock**
2 lbs. **bacon**
3 large **onions, finely minced**
6 **carrots, finely minced**
6 **celery stalks, finely minced**
1/2 lb. **smoked ham, finely chopped**
pepper to taste
1 cup **heavy cream**

Pour split peas, water and chicken stock into 10- to 12-quart stock pot and bring to boil. Boil 2 minutes. Remove from heat and let stand 1 hour. Fry bacon until crispy, then crumble; reserve a few tablespoons of bacon fat. Sauté onions, ham, carrots and celery in reserved bacon fat with crumbled bacon until tender. Add to peas and bring to a boil. Reduce heat and simmer about 1 hour. Add pepper if desired. Just before serving, stir in cream.

Serves 24.

SALMONBERRIES & CREAM MUFFINS

Bonnie Barrett
Wildflour Coffee Shop
Hyder, AK

Muffins:
3 1/2 cups **flour**
2/3 cup **granulated sugar**
5 tsp. **baking powder**
1/2 tsp. **salt**
2 **eggs, beaten**
1 1/2 cups **half and half**
2/3 cup **canola or vegetable oil**
2 cups **fresh-picked salmonberries**

Crumb mixture:
1/4 cup **granulated sugar**
1/4 cup **flour**
3 Tbs. **butter**

Preheat oven to 375°F. Grease a large, 12-cup muffin tin.
Whisk dry ingredients together and set aside. Whisk egg,
half and half and oil together. Stir into dry ingredients until
flour is just moistened. Gently fold in salmonberries. Divide
mixture evenly among the 12 cups.

In a small bowl, add sugar and flour and cut in butter. Mix
together until crumbly. Sprinkle over muffins. Bake about 25
minutes or until knife inserted into center comes out clean.

Yields 12 muffins.

Klondike Loop

The Klondike Loop is an alternate route to Alaska via Dawson City, YT. This route turns off the Alaska Highway just west of Whitehorse, heading north past the Keno-Mayo mining area to the historic Klondike gold fields and Yukon's first capital, Dawson City. Motorists cross the Yukon River by ferry at Dawson City, then follow the Top of the World Highway into Alaska, where the Taylor Highway takes them back to the Alaska Highway just outside Tok.

FRIENDSHIP TEA
Tracie Harris
Mom's Sourdough Bakery
Mile J 20.1 Klondike Loop

"This tea makes a great change from coffee."

1 1/2 cups **instant tea**
1 3-oz. package **orange drink crystals**
1 30-oz. package **lemonade crystals**
1 cup **granulated sugar**
1/2 tsp. **nutmeg**
1 tsp. **cinnamon**
1/2 tsp. **ground cloves**

Mix all ingredients well. Store in container. Add 2 teaspoons of mixture to boiling water.

Yields 65 8-oz. cups.

IRISH CREAM

Tracie Harris
Mom's Sourdough Bakery
Mile J 20.1 Klondike Loop

2 cups **whiskey**
1 can **Eagle® brand sweetened condensed milk**
2 Tbs. **HERSHEY's® chocolate syrup**
2 Tbs. **almond extract**
1 cup **whipping cream**
4 **eggs**
1 Tbs. **vanilla**
1 tsp. **instant coffee**

Blend all ingredients until well-mixed. This recipe will keep in the refrigerator for 2 months.

Serves 10 to 12.

CHICKEN & VEGETABLE ROTINI

Tracie Harris
Mom's Sourdough Bakery
Mile J 20.1 Klondike Loop

1 Tbs. **oil**
1 lb. **boneless chicken breasts, cut into chunks**
1 10-oz. (284 ml) **can cream of celery soup**
2 1/2 cups **water**
2 cups **frozen vegetables**
1/2 tsp. **dried basil leaves**
2 cups **rotini pasta, uncooked**

Heat oil at medium-high in large skillet. Add chicken and stir fry until cooked. Mix together soup, water, vegetables and basil and stir into chicken. Bring mixture to a boil, stirring often. Stir in pasta. Cook on medium-low heat until pasta is tender, stirring often. Serve with grated cheese if desired.

Serves 4.

CRUNCHY JAPANESE SALAD

Tracie Harris
Mom's Sourdough Bakery
Mile J 20.1 Klondike Loop

"Without a constant supply of fresh produce for salad making, we use this tangy salad as a standby."

1 medium **red cabbage**
1 package **Ichibon noodles**
$1/2$ cup **roasted almonds**
$1/4$ cup **sesame seeds**
$1/2$ cup **salad oil**
2 Tbs. **granulated sugar**
2 Tbs. **vinegar**
salt and pepper to taste

Shred cabbage and mix with crushed noodles, almonds and sesame seeds.

Mix together salad oil, sugar, vinegar, salt and pepper and seasoning from package of noodles. Pour mixture over cabbage mixture and marinate for 2 hours. Serve cold.

Serves 4 to 6.

HEART SMART POTATO TOPPING

Tracie Harris
Mom's Sourdough Bakery
Mile J 20.1 Klondike Loop

"This topping may be used on cooked veggies or as a sauce or low-calorie dip with raw veggies."

1/2 cup **plain, low-fat yogurt**
1 Tbs. **light mayonnaise**
1 tsp. **curry powder**

Mix all ingredients. Refrigerate and allow flavors to mix prior to use.

Serves 4 to 6.

SKINNY FRENCH FRIES

Tracie Harris
Mom's Sourdough Bakery
Mile J 20.1 Klondike Loop

"Taste and texture of French fries…but without the fat."

4 **medium potatoes**
1 Tbs. **oil**
$1/2$ tsp. **salt**
$1/2$ tsp. **paprika**

Preheat oven to 450°F. Cut potatoes lengthwise into $1/2$"-thick strips. While cutting, place strips in a bowl of ice water to keep them crisp. Drain the strips, pat them dry and put them into a dry bowl. Sprinkle with oil and mix with hands. Spread strips on baking sheet. Bake 30 to 40 minutes, turning frequently. Sprinkle with paprika and salt.

Serves 2 to 3.

SOURDOUGH CHOCOLATE CAKE

Tracie Harris
Mom's Sourdough Bakery
Mile J 20.1 Klondike Loop

Sourdough:
1/2 cup **thick sourdough starter** *(see recipe on page 107)*
1 1/2 cups **flour**
1 cup **water**
1/4 cup **non-fat dry milk**

Cake:
1 cup **granulated sugar**
1/2 cup **shortening**
1/2 tsp. **salt**
1 tsp. **vanilla**
1 tsp. **cinnamon**
1 1/2 tsp. **baking soda**
2 **eggs**
3 **squares unsweetened chocolate, melted**

Let sourdough ferment in a warm place until bubbly, 2 to 3 hours. Cream sugar, shortening, salt, vanilla, cinnamon and baking soda. Add eggs one at a time, beating well after each egg. Combine cream mixture with melted chocolate and sourdough. Stir for 300 strokes, or mix on low speed in blender until well blended. Pour into two layer pans or one 9" square pan. Bake at 350°F for 25 to 30 minutes. Cool, then frost with butterscotch chocolate frosting *(recipe follows)*.

Serves 8 to 10.

Butterscotch-Chocolate Frosting:
3 1-oz. squares **unsweetened chocolate**
$^1/_3$ cup **butter or margarine**
$^1/_2$ cup **light cream**
$^2/_3$ cup **packed brown sugar**
1 tsp. **vanilla**
3 cups **confectioner's sugar**

Combine chocolate, butter, cream and brown sugar in
saucepan. Bring to a boil and stir constantly. Cook until
chocolate is melted. Remove from heat and add vanilla and
enough confectioner's sugar for spreading consistency
(about 3 cups). Spread evenly over top and sides of cake.

ZUCCHINI CASSEROLE

Tracie Harris
Mom's Sourdough Bakery
Mile J 20.1 Klondike Loop

1 medium zucchini
3 to 4 ripe tomatoes
1 large onion
shredded Mozzarella cheese (or any favorite cheese) to garnish
salt, pepper and basil to season

Slice zucchini and tomatoes thinly. In a casserole dish (any size), layer zucchini, tomatoes and onions starting with zucchini. Continue layering until dish is full and season to taste. Bake at 350°F until vegetables are tender. Top with a layer of cheese.

Serves 4 to 12.

FOCACCIA FLAT BREAD

Bob and Edith MacAdam
Cranberry Point Cabins
and Bed and Breakfast
Mile J 29.4 Klondike Loop

2 cups **flour**
$1/2$ tsp. **salt**
1 Tbs. **instant yeast**
$3/4$ cup **very hot water**
1 Tbs. **olive oil**
coarse salt and herbs (your choice) to season

Mix together flour, salt and yeast. Mix oil and water, then add dry ingredients and stir together until dough leaves side of bowl. Knead gently, cover and let rise for $1/2$ hour. Punch dough down and divide in half. Knead each half into a round about $1/2$" thick, 8" or 9" diameter. Press dough with fingers to make dimples. Brush 2 Tbs. of olive oil on each round. Sprinkle with coarse salt and your choice of dry herbs. Bake at 425°F for 20 minutes.

Yields 2 8" to 10" round loaves.

HOBO BREAD
Bob and Edith MacAdam
Cranberry Point Cabins
and Bed and Breakfast
Mile J 29.4 Klondike Loop

"This is a non-dairy and low-fat bread."

2 cups **raisins**
4 tsp. **baking soda**
boiling water to cover raisins
2 cups **granulated sugar**
$1/2$ tsp. **salt**
4 Tbs. **oil**
4 cups **flour**
2 tsp. **almond extract**

Cover raisins and baking soda with boiling water and soak overnight (about 12 hours). Add sugar, salt, oil, flour and almond extract. Grease and flour 3 small tube pans and fill half full with dough. Bake at 350°F for about 1 hour.

Yields 3 small loaves.

Sweet Red Pepper Sauté

Bob and Edith MacAdam
Cranberry Point Cabins
and Bed and Breakfast
Mile J 29.4 Klondike Loop

"Sometimes you want a colorful side dish that is delicious too. This one fills both bills and is quick and easy."

2 Tbs. **olive oil**
$1/2$ cup **leeks, sliced**
1 $1/2$ cups **red pepper, sliced (1 large pepper)**
1 cup **zucchini, sliced $1/2$" thick**

In a large frying pan, heat oil and sauté leeks for 2 minutes. Add red pepper and sauté another 5 minutes. Add zucchini and sauté until tender. Serve hot.

Serves about 6.

CURRIED WINTER VEGETABLE & BEAN SOUP

Bob and Edith MacAdam
Cranberry Point Cabins
and Bed and Breakfast
Mile J 29.4 Klondike Loop

"Great the next day!"

1 Tbs. vegetable oil
1 large onion, chopped
2 cloves garlic, minced
1 tsp. fresh ginger, minced
1 Tbs. curry powder
4 cups chicken stock
1 small can tomatoes, drained and crushed
1 potato, diced
1 carrot, diced
1 can kernel corn (or 1 cup frozen corn)
1 small can canned beans (red, white, pinto, black-eyed, etc.),
   drained
2 Tbs. fresh parsley, chopped
salt and pepper to taste

In a heavy, 4-quart pot, heat oil. Add onions until softened. Add remaining ingredients in order up to parsley. When potatoes and carrots are tender, add parsley. Adjust salt and pepper to taste, and serve.

Serves 4 to 6.

KLONDIKE KATE'S FAMOUS TIN ROOF PIE

Wade LaMarche
Klondike Kate's
Dawson City, YT

2 cups **crushed corn flakes**
$1/4$ cup **peanut butter**
$1/4$ cup **corn syrup**
$1/3$ gallon **vanilla ice cream**
hot fudge sauce
whipped cream
peanuts, finely chopped

Mix corn flakes, peanut butter and corn syrup until flakes are well-coated. Press into pie plate to form crust. Fill with ice cream, and freeze. Once frozen, slice and serve. Top with hot fudge sauce, whipped cream and chopped peanuts.

Serves 8.

Glenn Highway

The Tok Cutoff and Glenn Highway form the most direct route from the Alaska Highway to Anchorage, Alaska's largest city. Like so many other Northern roads, this 328-mile-long highway follows the path of the early-day explorers and gold seekers through an almost unchanged landscape of mountains, glaciers, river valleys and forest. Scenic viewpoints dot this modern paved highway with its spectacular views of the Chugach and Wrangell mountains.

Crystal McEuen, manager of Mentasta Lodge, cooks, bakes and does "just about everything that needs to be done when needed."

She says: "We were the lodge right on top of the fault of the November 3, 2002, 7.9 earthquake located on the Tok Cutoff (yes, it's OUR fault). We are located as far as you could get on the road (after the quake). We had people from the highway at the lodge overnight. Linda (the lodge owner) made it out of the lodge, only to almost get run over by her own car. One good thing–the quake increased our satellite reception by 19 percent.

"One of the most interesting things we learned in the month or so after the quake was how our bodies reacted to dumping adrenaline into our systems (which happened sometimes several times a day during the hundreds of aftershocks that followed). When your body dumps adrenaline, it strips you of available sugar for energy (which was used in taking the shortest route out of the building). We craved sugar–lots of sugar. And our Quarter-pounder peanut butter cookies and pecan pralines seemed to do the trick. These two recipes were a hit during the aftershocks…and still are.

"Remember…we were the little lodge that could…and did!"

(Photos courtesy of Shannan & Wilson, Inc., Fairbanks, AK)

PECAN PRALINES

Crystal McEuen, Mentasta Lodge
Mile GJ 78.1 Tok Cutoff

"This is one of the easiest praline recipes I have ever worked with, and it doesn't take near the amount of ingredients or time most of them do.
  Use at least a 4-quart pan for these, a 6-quart would be even better."

3 cups **granulated sugar**
1 tsp. **baking soda**
1 12-oz. can **evaporated milk**

2 Tbs. **butter or margarine**
2 cups **pecans**

In a heavy-bottomed, 4- or 6-quart saucepan, mix sugar and baking soda. When well-mixed, add evaporated milk. Place over medium heat, stirring constantly until mixture comes to a boil. Turn heat to very low and cook until it reaches 240°F. Mixture will foam up, which is normal; make sure it does not boil over (why the larger pan is better!) Stir frequently (a wooden spoon works best), scraping the crust on the side of the pan. (But don't try to get it all, and don't butter the side of the pan to prevent it from forming.) When candy reaches 240°F, remove from stove and add butter or margarine and pecans. Stir until candy starts to thicken slightly. Drop by spoonfuls onto waxed paper. You can make these as large or as small as you wish. Remove each piece from waxed paper when firm and store in a tightly covered container.

"And an added bonus: the pan will look like you should throw it away, but just fill with hot water and let sit about 10 minutes, and it will wash right out.
  "If you cook this until it reaches 215° to 220°F and finish, it makes the most wonderful topping for butter pecan ice cream ever!
  "We hope you enjoy these as much as we do."

QUARTER POUNDER
PEANUT BUTTER COOKIES

Crystal McEuen, Mentasta Lodge
Mile GJ 78.1 Tok Cutoff

2 sticks **margarine**
1 cup **granulated sugar**
1 cup **brown sugar**
1 Tbs. **vanilla**
2 **eggs**
2 cups **peanut butter (smooth or crunchy)**
1 tsp. **baking powder**
1 tsp. **baking soda**
2 tsp. **salt**
2 to 2 ¹/2 cups **all-purpose flour**

Beat margarine and sugars in a mixing bowl until light and creamy. Add vanilla and eggs and continue to beat until fluffy. Add peanut butter, baking powder, baking soda and salt. Mix until blended. Add flour. (Dough should form a slightly firm ball without being crumbly.) Divide dough into 12 equal portions (about 5 oz. each, or use a #6 ice cream scoop overfilled a bit), and form into balls. Place on a full-sized baking sheet and flatten slightly. Crisscross with tines of a fork, pressing lightly. Bake at 375°F for 17 minutes or until lightly browned on edges. Cookies will be very soft when taken out of oven. Cool on pan until firm.

"I have never tried to make normal-sized cookies with this recipe, but a regular cookie sheet will hold 4. The dough freezes well. Shape into balls and double wrap in plastic film or Saran wrap. Be sure to bring to room temperature before continuing."

Spiced Blueberry Jam

Gary and Maraley McMichael
Nabesna House B&B
Mile J 0.8 Nabesna Road

7 8-oz. **jelly jars with lids and bands**
5 cups **fresh or frozen blueberries, crushed**
1 cup **water**
2 Tbs. **lemon juice**

$^1/_2$ tsp. **ground cinnamon**
$^1/_2$ tsp. **ground cloves**
$^1/_4$ tsp. **butter**
1 package **Ball® Fruit Jell® No Sugar Needed pectin**
3 cups **granulated sugar**

Wash jars, lids and bands. Place jars upright in 9" X 13" glass dish ready to fill with boiling water. Place lids and bands in saucepan. Cover with hot water and keep hot over low heat. Fill teakettle and bring to boil. Prepare and measure fruit into a 6- to 8-quart saucepan. Add water, lemon juice, spices and butter. Measure and set aside sugar. Gradually stir pectin into prepared fruit using a wire whisk (do not add all at once). Bring to a boil over high heat, stirring constantly. Just before jam boils, turn off heat long enough to pour boiling water over jars. Stir sugar into boiling fruit mixture and return to boil. Boil hard 1 minute, stirring constantly. Remove from heat and skim foam if necessary. (The butter reduces foam.) Empty water from jars and turn upside down on sterile towel for 30 seconds to drain. Upright jars and carefully ladle or pour jam into jars, leaving $^1/_4$" headspace. Wipe jar edge and clean with wet, sterile cloth. Place metal lids on jars and screw on bands. Process jars 10 minutes in a boiling water bath canner. Remove jars and let cool. Make sure lids are sealed (lid should not spring up when center is pressed) and store jam in refrigerator.

Yields 6 to 7 jars.

COCONUT/GINGER BAKED HALIBUT

Jodi Talcott
Majestic Valley Wilderness Lodge
Mile A 114.9 Glenn Highway

"This is an easy topping to prepare and adds a light, zingy taste to freshly caught Alaskan halibut. I serve this with Basmati rice and stir-fried vegetables."

12 serving-size portions of halibut (I get the full skinned fillets and cut them into the desired serving size).
4 Tbs. olive oil
2 yellow or white onions, finely chopped
2 2/3 cups shredded coconut
4" piece of ginger root, peeled and chopped
5 cloves garlic, finely chopped
4 jalapeño peppers, seeded and finely chopped
1 tsp. chili powder
zest of 2 lemons
juice of 2 lemons

Lay halibut on a baking tray and refrigerate until topping is complete.

In a wok or large stir fry pan, combine oil, onions, coconut, ginger root, garlic and jalapeño peppers. Add chili powder, lemon juice and lemon zest and sauté about another 5 minutes. Place the topping on the halibut fillets. Bake at 375°F for about 20 to 25 minutes, depending on the thickness of the halibut. The topping will be golden brown and slightly crunchy on top. Garnish with fresh cilantro.

Serves 12.

TOMATO BRUSCHETTA

Jodi Talcott
Majestic Valley Wilderness Lodge
Mile A 114.9 Glenn Highway

"This bruschetta is great in the summer served on toasted garlic bread."

3 large tomatoes or 10 small tomatoes, diced 1/4"
3 cloves garlic, minced
6 Greek olives, minced
3/4 cup red onion, finely chopped
1/4 cup balsamic vinegar
1/3 cup olive oil
2 tsp. fresh basil, finely chopped
salt and pepper to season
French bread
fresh basil to garnish

Mix all ingredients together. Season with salt and pepper. Slice French bread and brush with olive oil. Sprinkle slices with freshly minced garlic, and toast. Place bruschetta on toast right before serving, as the bread will get soggy if it sits too long. Garnish platter with fresh basil leaves.

Serves 10 to 12.

CORN CHOWDER

Zack and Anjanette Steer
Sheep Mountain Lodge
Mile A 113.5 Glenn Highway

"This recipe is a guest favorite after a long day hiking or skiing. It is good as a main dish or appetizer soup for a seafood meal."

2 Tbs. butter
2 medium onions, finely chopped
4 celery stalks, finely chopped
2 cloves of garlic, minced
12 cups whole milk
1 large potato, peeled and diced
1 Tbs. salt
1 Tbs. ground black pepper
1 bag frozen kernel corn
1 Tbs. parsley, finely chopped

Using a large soup pot, sauté onions, celery and garlic in butter until tender and slightly browned. Add milk and potatoes. Bring milk to a slow boil, reduce heat and simmer, covered, until potatoes are tender (about 15 to 20 minutes).

Stir in salt, pepper and $^1/2$ bag of kernel corn. After soup is cooked, purée approximately $^3/4$ of the solids in a food processor or blender and add back to soup. Add remaining whole kernel corn and parsley to pot. Add additional salt and pepper to taste. Stir well to prevent scorching.

Note: A meat version of this soup can easily be made by adding 10 slices of crispy cooked bacon (chopped) and 2 Tbs. of bacon grease (omit butter used to sauté) to the pot before sautéing onions.

SMOKED SALMON SPREAD

Zack and Anjanette Steer
Sheep Mountain Lodge
Mile A 113.5 Glenn Highway

"An excellent spread for fresh-baked French bread or even spread thinly with lettuce and tomato on sandwich bread for sack lunches on a long-day's hike. The cayenne pepper and garlic powder give the spread a little bit of kick."

18 oz. **cream cheese, softened to room temperature**
1/2 **filet of smoked salmon, de-boned (We always use Alaska Sausage brand smoked salmon.)**
1/4 tsp. **cayenne pepper**
1/2 tsp. **garlic powder**
1 tsp. **dried parsley**
1 tsp. **dill weed**
dried parsley to garnish
Parmesan cheese to garnish

Blend all ingredients in food processor to desired consistency and chill. For a chunkier version, mix half of the salmon in with a spoon after all other ingredients have been blended.

Garnish with parsley flakes and fresh grated Parmesan cheese. Serve with sliced French baguette.

For special events, place spread in a metal fish mold (lined with plastic wrap) before refrigerating.

Serves about 10.

ALASKAN WILD RASPBERRY SAUCE FOR SALMON

The Dietrich Family
Grand View Café & RV Campground
Mile A 109.7 Glenn Highway

"I use homemade jam from Alaska wild raspberries. This sauce is fabulous over poached, barbecued or grilled salmon."

1/2 cup **raspberry wine**
1/4 cup **minced green onion**
4 Tbs. **whipping cream**
1/2 cup **butter**
2 Tbs. **raspberry jam**

Cook raspberry wine with green onions until reduced to 2 tablespoons. Add cream and stir over low heat until once again reduced to 2 tablespoons. Add butter and continue to stir over low heat until thickened. Add jam and stir until blended.

Yields about 2 cups.

Roasted Red Pepper and Artichoke Torta

Colleen Dietrich
Tundra Rose Bed & Breakfast
Mile A 109.5 Glenn Highway

2 8-oz. packages **cream cheese**
1 packet (1 oz.) **Hidden Valley® Original Ranch® Salad Dressing mix**
1 6-oz. jar **marinated artichoke hearts, drained and chopped**
$1/3$ cup **roasted red peppers, drained and chopped**
3 Tbs. **fresh parsley, minced**

Cream the cream cheese and dressing mix together. In a separate bowl, stir together artichokes, peppers and parsley. In a 3-cup bowl lined with plastic wrap, alternate layers of cheese and vegetable mixtures—beginning and ending with cheese layer. Chill 4 hours. Invert onto plate and remove plastic wrap. Serve with crackers.

Serves 10 to 12.

Schwabenkraut Salad

Chef Bill Weith
Schwabenhof
Mile W 2.4 Palmer-Wasilla Highway

"People just love this stuff," Bill Weith says of this tasty German-style salad. "It's great served with bratwurst and beer."

32 oz. **sauerkraut** (store-bought or homemade)
1 **red bell pepper**, finely diced
1 **yellow bell pepper**, finely diced
1 **yellow onion**, finely diced
1/2 cup **canola oil**
1/2 cup **white vinegar**
1/2 cup **granulated sugar**

Mix sauerkraut (including the liquid) and vegetables in large glass or heavy plastic bowl (see note below). In empty sauerkraut jar, mix oil, vinegar and sugar and shake vigorously. Pour mixture over salad. Cover bowl with plastic (see note below) and refrigerate for 48 hours.

About this trademark salad, Bill notes: "Be sure to use a glass or heavy plastic bowl, never aluminum or any other metal, and never cover it with foil. The wrong container with mess up this salad."

Serves 6 to 8.

Schwabenhof, Bill Weith's octagonal, handcrafted log restaurant/bar, high on a hill 2.4 miles east of Wasilla, is a favorite gathering place for lovers of hearty German food, 18 outstanding on-tap beers and a spectacular view.

Anchorage

Fly By Night Club
Harley's Old Thyme Café
Kincaid Grill
Millennium Hotel
Walkabout Town Bed & Breakfast

A modern metropolis perched on the edge of a wilderness, Anchorage has sometimes been described as being located "half an hour from Alaska." It is Alaska's largest city, situated on a broad peninsula between Cook Inlet's Knik Arm and Turnagain Arm, with the rugged Chugach Mountains forming the eastern boundary of the city. Anchorage is located at the end of both the Glenn and Seward highways, and is a hub for air, rail, cruise ship and highway travelers.

The zany seasonal musicals at the Fly By Night Club in the slightly seedy Spenard district have been a bright spot on the Anchorage nightclub scene for more than 20 years. Accompanied by a group of talented musicians, Mr. Whitekeys and his wacky cast make fun of everything from Alaska politics to our predilection for Spam® ("Alaskans are the 2nd highest per capita consumers of Spam® in the nation").

"Usually you can find Spam® on our menu, but sometimes we wipe it off," says Mr. Whitekeys.

Actually, the Fly By Night Club serves a wide selection of Spam® dishes. There's Coconut Beer Batter Spam®, Spam® Nachos, Spam® Burgers, Spam® Dijonnaise and the fabulous Chipotle Spamadillas (recipe follows).

Mr. Whitekeys reminds first-time Fly By Night Club customers: "Ask for the 'Frequent Spammer' card. If you eat 10 Spam® dishes, you get the next one FREE!"

CHIPOTLE SPAMADILLAS

Mr. Whitekeys'
Fly By Night Club
~~Anchorage~~ Spenard, AK

1 cup **diced Spam®**
1/2 cup **red onion, julienned**
1/4 cup **green pepper, julienned**
1/4 cup **red pepper, julienned**
2 Tbs. **chipotle butter**
  (recipe follows)
splash **white wine**

1 to 2 Tbs. **canola or peanut oil**
2 10" **flour tortillas**
8 oz. **cheddar cheese, grated**
4 Tbs. **diced green chilies**
sour cream **to garnish**
guacamole **to garnish**
salsa **to garnish**

In a frying pan, sauté Spam® and julienned vegetables in chipotle butter until Spam® is lightly browned and vegetables are softened. Deglaze with a splash of white wine. Coat another frying pan with 1 to 2 Tbs. of light cooking oil. Rub tortillas in the pan to spread oil, and evenly coat each tortilla. Remove tortillas from pan and allow pan to reach medium-high heat.

Spread cheddar cheese, chilies and Spam® mixture on tortillas. Fold tortillas, and place them in the pan. Cook until cheese is melted. Garnish with salsa, sour cream and guacamole.

Yields 2 large Spamadillas.
Serves 2 entrée portions or 4 to 6 hors d'ouevres portions.

Chipotle Butter:
2 Tbs. **canned chipotle chilies en adobo, pureed**
2 cloves **garlic, finely minced**
1 stick **softened butter**
4 tsp. **fresh cilantro, chopped**
2 tsp. **fresh lime juice**
2 tsp. **tequila**
salt and pepper to taste

Puree chipotle chilies with sauce. In a mixing bowl, combine minced garlic, butter and chipotle puree until mixture is smooth. Add cilantro, lime juice and tequila and stir or beat until uniformly blended. Add salt and pepper to taste.

MR. KEYS' COOLER

Mr. Whitekeys'
Fly By Night Club
~~Anchorage~~ Spenard, AK

1 1/4 oz. light Puerto Rican rum
1 1/2 oz. purple grape juice
3 oz. cranberry juice cocktail
About 10 oz. ginger ale
juice of 1/4 lemon
lemon wedge for garnish

In a tall 16-oz. tumbler or chimney glass, combine rum, grape juice and cranberry juice cocktail over ice. Fill nearly to top with ginger ale. Squeeze lemon juice into cocktail and garnish with fresh lemon wedge.

Mr. Keys' Cooler is also served without rum as a Fly By Night Club nonalcoholic special.

After pleasing the clientele for 15 years at the cafeteria of an Anchorage hospital, Harley Livingston opened his own restaurant. Loyal longtime customers flock to Harley's Old Thyme Café on 76th Avenue and Old Seward Highway. Go early if you want a good seat for his Sunday morning brunch.

GERMAN CHOCOLATE PIE

Harley Livingston
Harley's Old Thyme Café
Anchorage, AK

$1/4$ cup **butter**
1 4-oz. package **German sweet chocolate**
1 $1/2$ cups **evaporated milk**
1 $1/2$ cups **granulated sugar**
3 Tbs. **cornstarch**
pinch **of salt**
2 **eggs**
1 tsp. **vanilla**
1 **unbaked pastry shell or pie crust**
1 $1/3$ cups **flaked coconut**
$1/2$ cup **pecans, chopped**

Melt butter and chocolate over low heat. Blend well. Remove from heat and gradually add milk. In a separate bowl, mix sugar, cornstarch and salt. Beat together eggs and vanilla and gradually blend into chocolate mixture. Pour into unbaked pastry shell or pie crust. Mix coconut and pecans and sprinkle over filling. Bake at 375°F for 45 minutes until set.

OLD FASHIONED MEATLOAF

Harley Livingston
Harley's Old Thyme Café
Anchorage, AK

3/4 cup **milk**
3 slices **white bread**
5 lbs. **ground beef**
4 oz. **onion, chopped**
1/4 cup **celery, chopped**
1/4 cup **bell pepper, chopped**
1 1/2 Tbs. **salt**
1/2 tsp. **black pepper**
1/2 tsp. **garlic powder**
2 **eggs**

Soften bread in milk. Add all ingredients and mix well. Shape into loaf and bake at 350°F for 45 minutes to 1 hour until done.

Serves 10 to 16.

Chef Al Levinsohn's Kincaid Grill at "Four Corners," the intersection of Jewel Lake and Raspberry roads, specializes in Alaska regional cuisine. His original seafood dishes are presented daily at this popular restaurant as well as on his weekly, early-morning television show.

OYSTERS CASINO
Chef Al Levinsohn
Kincaid Grill
Anchorage, AK

^{1}/4 cup **unsalted butter, softened**
1 Tbs. **shallots, finely minced**
1 Tbs. **finely minced garlic**
^{1}/4 cup **celery, finely minced**
^{1}/4 cup **green bell pepper, finely minced**
^{1}/4 cup **plain bread crumbs**
^{1}/4 cup **Parmesan cheese, grated**
1 ^{1}/2 Tbs. **fresh lemon juice**

2 Tbs. **parsley, chopped**
Kosher salt to taste
fresh-ground black pepper to taste
rock salt
24 **Alaska oysters, shucked and on the half shell**
24 **par-cooked bacon strips, 1" strips**

Melt butter over low heat. Add shallots, garlic, celery and peppers. Cook over low heat until tender. Remove from heat and add bread crumbs, Parmesan, lemon juice and parsley. Season to taste with salt and pepper. Preheat oven to 450°F.

Line the bottom of an oven-safe baking dish with rock salt about ^{1}/2" deep. Place oysters on rock salt to keep upright. Divide mixture evenly over oysters. Top mixture with bacon. Bake in oven until bacon becomes crispy, about 5 to 7 minutes. Serve hot.

Serves 4.

CHEF AL'S GUMBO

Chef Al Levinsohn
Kincaid Grill
Anchorage, AK

1 cup **vegetable oil**
1 1/2 cups **flour**
3/4 cup **green bell peppers, diced**
3/4 cup **onions, diced**
3/4 cup **celery, diced**
1 lb. **Andoullie sausage**
1 lb. **chicken thigh meat, diced**
6 cups **chicken broth**
gumbo seasoning to taste (recipe follows)
1 lb. **large shrimp, shelled**
2 cups **rice, steamed**
green onions, minced for garnish

In a large cast iron Dutch oven or heavy-gauge soup pot, heat oil until it begins to smoke. Add flour, and immediately begin stirring. Be careful, as the flour will create steam when it comes in contact with the hot oil. Continue stirring the roux constantly, scraping the sides and bottom of the pot to ensure no black specks appear. If black specks appear, you must start over. Roux should be smooth with consistent color throughout. Cook roux to the color of an old penny. Remove from heat and add vegetables. (Be careful, as they will produce a lot of steam.) Sweat vegetables in roux until tender. Add sausage, chicken and hot chicken stock. Bring to a full boil and reduce to simmer, skimming foam as necessary. Simmer for about 45 minutes to cook out taste of the flour. Season to taste with gumbo seasoning, adding a small amount at a time until desired heat level is achieved.

Just prior to serving, add shrimp and cook just until shrimp are firm, approximately 4 minutes. Serve with steamed rice and fresh chopped scallions.

Serves 8.

Gumbo Seasoning:
1 Tbs. **cayenne pepper**
1 Tbs. **white pepper**
1 Tbs. **black pepper**
1 Tbs. **thyme**
1 Tbs. **basil**

Mix seasonings together well.

SHRIMP AND WILD MUSHROOM PASTA

Chef Al Levinsohn
Kincaid Grill
Anchorage, AK

2 Tbs. olive oil
1 lb. shrimp, peeled and de-veined
4 oz. wild mushrooms, chopped
2 Tbs. fresh garlic, chopped
2 oz. chicken or fish stock
3 cups heavy cream
4 egg yolks
6 oz. Parmesan cheese, grated
salt and pepper to taste
1 lb. fresh pasta, cooked
fresh parsley, chopped to garnish

Bring an 8-quart pot of lightly salted water to a boil. In a large sauté pan, heat oil until a light haze forms. Add shrimp and mushrooms and cook over medium heat. Add garlic and heat through. De-glaze pan with stock. Combine cream and eggs and add to sauté pan. Heat mixture until just before boiling point. Stir in Parmesan cheese, and season with salt and white pepper to taste. Toss with fresh cooked pasta and garnish with parsley.

Serves 4.

STEAMED MUSSELS WITH FRESH HERBS

Chef Al Levinsohn
Kincaid Grill
Anchorage, AK

1/4 cup **olive oil**
2 Tbs. **shallots, finely minced**
2 Tbs. **finely minced garlic**
4 oz. **Andouille sausage**
1 lb. **Pacific mussels (beards removed)**
1/2 cup **white wine**
1/2 cup **tomatoes, diced**
1/4 cup **fresh herbs, chopped (oregano, thyme, basil, parsley)**
1/4 cup **whole butter**
2 Tbs. **fresh lemon juice**
salt and pepper to taste

Heat olive oil over medium heat. Add shallots, garlic and sausage. Sauté until heated through. Add mussels and white wine. Cover and cook until mussels have opened. Add tomatoes, herbs, butter and lemon juice and toss to combine. Season to taste with salt and black pepper. Serve immediately.

Serves 4.

BLACKENED PRAWNS/SALMON/SCALLOPS

Lastan Williams, Executive Chef
Millennium Hotel
Anchorage, AK

3/4 lb. (3 sticks) **unsalted butter**
1 lb. **jumbo prawns, or** 6 **salmon (or other fish) filets,**
  or 2 lbs. **fresh sea scallops**

Seasoning Mix:

1 Tbs. **sweet paprika**	3/4 tsp. **white pepper**
2 1/2 tsp. **salt**	3/4 tsp. **black pepper**
1 tsp. **onion powder**	1/2 tsp. **dry thyme leaves**
1 tsp. **garlic powder**	1/2 tsp. **dry oregano leaves**
1 tsp. **cayenne pepper**	

Melt butter in a skillet. Heat a large cast iron skillet over very high heat until it's beyond the smoking stage, at least 10 minutes, and you see white ash in the skillet bottom (the skillet cannot be too hot for this dish).

Thoroughly combine seasoning mix ingredients in a small bowl. Dip each prawn/filet/scallop in the melted butter, so both sides are well coated. Sprinkle seasoning mix generously and evenly over both sides of prawns/filets/scallops, patting it in with your hand. Place in the hot skillet, and pour 1/4 tsp. melted butter over each prawn/filet/scallop. (Be careful; butter may flame up.) Cook, uncovered, over very high heat until underside of seafood looks charred, about 1 to 1 1/2 minutes (time will vary according to the thickness and heat of the skillet).

Turn the prawns/filets/scallops over and, again, pour $1/4$ tsp. butter over top. Cook until done. Repeat with remaining seafood.

Serve each portion (about 3 to 4) while piping hot. To serve prawns, pour Shrimp Creole Hollandaise on a plate, and top with prawns. To serve scallops or salmon, melt 2 Tbs. butter into 6 small ramekins. Place scallops or a filet and a ramekin of butter on each heated plate.

Serves 4 to 6.

Creole Shrimp Hollandaise Sauce

Hollandaise Sauce:
$1/2$ cup **butter**
1 $1/2$ Tbs. **lemon juice, dry sherry or tarragon vinegar**
4 Tbs. **water**
3 **egg yolks**
$1/4$ tsp. **salt**
small dash **of cayenne pepper**

Creole Shrimp:
$1/4$ cup **green onion, diced**
$1/4$ cup **Bay shrimp**
$1/4$ cup **ham, diced**
2 Tbs. **Cajun spice mix (available at grocery stores)**
$1/4$ cup **diced tomatoes**

Melt butter slowly, and keep it warm. Barely heat lemon juice, sherry or vinegar. Boil water. Place egg yolks in top of a double boiler over hot water. Beat yolks with a wire whisk until they begin to thicken. Add 1 Tbs. boiling water and beat again until eggs begin to thicken. Repeat process until you have added 3 more Tbs. of boiling water. Then, beat in warm lemon juice, sherry or vinegar. Remove double boiler from heat and beat sauce well with wire whisk. Continue to beat while slowly adding melted butter, salt and cayenne pepper. Beat until sauce is thick. Add Creole shrimp ingredients to sauce. Mix well and serve with steaks or seafood.

BLUEBERRY CHEESECAKE

Lastan Williams, Executive Chef
Millennium Hotel
Anchorage, AK

5 oz. **graham cracker crumbs**
2 oz. **butter (to coat pans)**
2 oz. **pecans, toasted and ground**
3 lbs. **cream cheese**
3 **egg yolks**
2 **whole eggs**
2 cups **granulated sugar**
$1/2$ cup **sour cream**
1 tsp. **vanilla extract**
3 Tbs. **flour**
$1/2$ cup **blueberries**

Preheat oven to 250°F. Prepare springform pan. Mix graham cracker crumbs, butter and toasted pecans and press into bottom of pan to form crust. Mix cream cheese until soft, then beat in eggs for 5 minutes, scraping the bowl. Beat in sugar, sour cream, vanilla and flour. Fold in blueberries. Pour into pans and bake for 1 hour and 15 minutes. Cool completely.

Serves 12 to 14.

CREAMY CHICKEN WITH ARTICHOKES & ROASTED PECANS

Lastan Williams, Executive Chef
Millennium Hotel
Anchorage, AK

1 lb. **butter**
1 cup **flour**
2 cups **water**
3 cups **half and half**
1 cup **celery, diced**
1 cup **carrots, diced**
1 cup **onions, diced**
2 Tbs. **granulated garlic**
1 tsp. **white pepper**
3 Tbs. **chicken base**
2 cups **chicken meat, cooked and diced**
1 cup **artichoke hearts, sliced**
3 Tbs. **cilantro, chopped**
1/2 cup **roasted pecans**

In a soup kettle, melt butter and add flour to make a roux. Add water and half and half. Then add celery, carrots and onions. Stir occasionally with a wire whisk. Season with garlic, pepper and chicken base. Turn down to medium heat and add chicken meat and sliced artichoke hearts. Simmer for 10 minutes. Add cilantro and garnish with roasted pecans.

Serves 4.

RASPBERRY VINAIGRETTE
Lastan Williams, Executive Chef
Millennium Hotel
Anchorage, AK

2 **egg yolks**
6 oz. **red wine vinegar**
2 oz. **Melba sauce**
2 oz. **raspberry puree (frozen pureed in processor)**
1/2 tsp. **garlic, minced**
2 oz. **granulated sugar**
6 oz. **salad oil**
6 oz. **olive oil**

Using a mixing bowl and wire whisk, mix egg yolks, vinegar, Melba sauce, raspberry puree, garlic and sugar for 1 minute. Mix salad and olive oils together and slowly add other ingredients while briskly whipping. Should be frothy in appearance with foam at top. For best results, use an electric mixer or food processor. Refrigerate.

SEAFOOD CHOWDER

Lastan Williams, Executive Chef
Millennium Hotel
Anchorage, AK

1 stick **of butter**
6 **celery stalks, diced**
1 **medium onion, diced**
1 tsp. **garlic**
$1/2$ Tbs. **fresh basil, chopped**
$1/2$ tsp. **dill weed**
1 tsp. **Italian seasoning**
$1/2$ tsp. **white pepper**
2 qts. **clam stock or juice**
1 lb. **chopped clams**
1 qt. **half and half**
2 lbs. **potatoes, diced**
1 lb. **fresh seafood (your choice), cooked and diced**

Melt butter in 2-gallon pot. Add celery and onions and
cook until soft. Add spices and stir for 2 minutes. Add clam
juice and clams and bring to simmer. Thicken with $1/4$ cup
potato or cornstarch mixed in $1/2$ cup water; add slowly,
stirring all the time. Add half and half to thin if needed.
Add potatoes and seafood.

Yields approximately 2 gallons.

RHUBARB MUFFINS

Sandy Stimson
Walkabout Town Bed & Breakfast
Anchorage, AK

1 box **Krusteaz**® brand oat bran muffin mix
$1/2$ cup **water**
1 cup **rhubarb sauce** *(recipe follows)*
$1/2$ cup **nuts (any kind), chopped**

Preheat oven to 400°F, and prepare a muffin pan by lightly spraying with cooking spray or by lining with paper baking cups. Follow muffin recipe on box, using only $1/2$ the water. (Mix $1/2$ cup water with full box of muffin mix. Stir until moistened.) Mix in rhubarb sauce and most of the nuts. (If mix is dry, add a little more water.) Pour mix into muffin cups or tins, filling $2/3$ full. Sprinkle each muffin with remaining nuts. Bake for 12 to 15 minutes (depending on muffin size). Muffins may need to bake longer than indicated due to the rhubarb sauce. When muffins are done, cool for 5 minutes on a wire rack and store in a tightly covered container.

Rhubarb Sauce:
8 cups **rhubarb, cut into 1 $1/2$" pieces**
4 cups **granulated sugar**

Mix rhubarb and sugar in a pot. Bring to a slow boil and taste. If sauce is too sour, add more sugar to taste. When rhubarb is broken down and sauce is the desired consistency, remove from heat, stir and cool.

Parks Highway

Completed in 1971, and formally named the George Parks Highway, the Parks Highway runs 362 miles through some of the grandest scenery that Alaska has to offer, crossing the Alaska Range at Broad Pass. The highway parallels the Alaska Railroad, connecting Anchorage and Fairbanks and providing the most direct highway access to Denali National Park. Mount McKinley, also called Denali, can be seen from many places along this highway, provided there's clear weather around North America's tallest peak.

FIDDLEHEAD FERN AND BACON QUICHE

Felix Zollinger, Executive Chef
Talkeetna Alaskan Lodge
Mile J 12.8 Talkeetna Spur Road

4 to 5 **bacon strips**
1/4 cup **garlic**
4 oz. **butter**
1/4 cup **yellow onions, chopped**
8 oz. **fiddlehead ferns, blanched**
1/4 cup **white wine (Savignon Blanc or Chenin Blanc)**
1/4 tsp. **fennel seed, roasted**
4 **large eggs**
1 cup **half and half**
pinch **cayenne pepper**
pinch **white pepper**
pinch **nutmeg**
6 oz. **Havarti cheese, shredded**
4 oz. **Parmesan cheese, shredded**
1 9" **pie shell, uncooked**

Cook and dice bacon. Roast garlic in olive oil and chop. In a frying pan, sauté butter, onions, ferns, white wine and fennel seed. Add bacon and garlic and set aside to cool. Mix in egg, half and half, peppers, nutmeg and cheeses. Test flavor and adjust ingredients to taste. Fill pie shell 3/4 full. Bake at 300°F for 35 to 40 minutes or until mixture is firm.

Yields 1 9" quiche.

JAPANESE MAYONNAISE DRESSING

Felix Zollinger, Executive Chef
Talkeetna Alaskan Lodge
Mile J 12.8 Talkeetna Spur Road

Ingredients for this recipe can be found at most Asian food markets.

$1/4$ **red onion, finely diced**
2 cloves **garlic, finely diced**
1 $1/2$ oz. **rice vinegar (seasoned)**
1 tube **Japanese Kewpie® mayonnaise**
1 tsp. **Dijon mustard**
1 Tbs. **Mae Ploy® sauce**
$1/2$ tsp. **ground black pepper**

In a bowl, mix all ingredients together. Serve with a seafood salad over romaine or iceberg lettuce.

Yields 2 cups.

Smoked Salmon Whiskey Bisque

Felix Zollinger, Executive Chef
Talkeetna Alaskan Lodge
Mile J 12.8 Talkeetna Spur Road

"By following these instructions step-by-step, you will be rewarded with accolades from your guests, and of course congratulations and compliments from myself are in order."

Smoked Salmon Stock:
2 Tbs. olive oil
2 to 3 lbs. hot smoked salmon collars, bellies or bones
1/4 cup carrots, peeled and coarsely cut
1/2 cup white onions, peeled and coarsely cut
2 cloves garlic, crushed
1/4 cup celery, chopped
1/4 cup brandy or cognac
1 bay leaf
1 Tbs. tarragon, dried or fresh
1/2 cup tomato paste
1 qt. cold water

Bisque:
4 oz. unsalted butter
3/4 cup flour
1 qt. salmon stock, heated
1/4 oz. fresh lemon juice
dash of Tabasco® brand hot sauce
1 Tbs. Worcestershire sauce (Lea & Perrins®)
1/4 tsp. Old Bay® seasoning
1/4 tsp. ground white pepper
3 cups heavy cream
3 tsp. whiskey (10 High Sour Mash)
2 Tbs. dry sherry
2 Tbs. unsalted butter, softened

For salmon stock: Heat oil in a large stockpot. Add salmon and all vegetables and brown lightly. Add brandy or cognac and ignite. When flames have expired, add bay leaf, tarragon and tomato paste. Mix well using a wooden spoon. Add water. Bring stock to a low simmer for about 2 hours. Strain through a fine sieve and keep hot. If stock needs to be refrigerated until making the bisque, it will need to be reheated.

For bisque: Make a roux in a heavy pot (large enough to hold 2 qts. of liquid), melting butter then adding flour, all at once. Stir with a whisk on low heat for about 5 minutes. Add salmon stock (cup by cup), whisking thoroughly after each addition. Bring to a boil and reduce to simmer for about 30 minutes. Add lemon juice, Tabasco®, Worcestershire sauce, Old Bay® seasoning and white pepper. Simmer for 10 minutes. Add cream, whiskey, sherry and butter and whisk briskly. Do not boil, and hold pot in a double boiler (water bath) until ready to serve. If desired, add hot smoked salmon flakes.

For a float/garnish for each bowl, spoon in 1 tsp. of whipped cream mixed with a touch of freshly chopped tarragon.

Serves 6 to 8.

BANANA WALNUT CHOCOLATE BREAD

Trisha Costello Zepf
Talkeetna Roadhouse
Talkeetna, AK

$1/2$ cup **butter, melted**
1 $1/4$ cups **granulated sugar**
2 **eggs**
1 $1/2$ cups **mashed bananas**
$1/2$ cup **buttermilk**
zest of $1/2$ an orange
2 $1/2$ cups **flour**
1 tsp. **baking soda**
1 tsp. **salt**
$1/2$ cup **chocolate chips**
$1/2$ cup **walnuts**

Cream butter and sugar, slowly adding in eggs, banana, buttermilk and zest. In a separate bowl, combine flour, baking soda and salt. Add this mixture to wet ingredients. Add chocolate chips and nuts. Spread mixture into greased and floured loaf pan. Bake at 350°F for 45 minutes. You may need to cover with foil for last 15 minutes of bake time. Loaf is done when toothpick inserted in middle comes out clean.

Serves 6 to 8.

MONSTER COOKIES

Trisha Costello Zepf
Talkeetna Roadhouse
Talkeetna, AK

"These cookies are great hot out of the oven and even better pulled out of the freezer for an out-on-the-trail snack."

2/3 cup **butter, melted**
1 1/4 cups **brown sugar**
3/4 cup **granulated sugar**
4 **eggs**
1 1/2 cups **peanut butter (Adams® Crunchy is best)**
2 tsp. **baking soda**
6 cups **oats**
2 cups **chocolate chips**
2 cups **raisins**

Cream butter and sugars together. Slowly add eggs one at a time. Add peanut butter. Mix baking soda with oats and add mixture to wet ingredients. Add chocolate chips and raisins. (At this point, mixing by hand is recommended.)

Use a large ice cream scoop (approximately 5 oz.) to place cookie balls onto greased cookie sheet. Flatten cookies to 1/2" thickness, making sure the edges are tucked in. The dough will be sticky. Bake at 350°F for 20 minutes. The edges should be just browning.

Yields 20 cookies.

PLANTAIN SOUP

Vilma Anderson
McKinley Foothills B&B and Cabins
Mile J 17.2 Petersville Road

$1/2$ lb. **pork meat with bones**
2 cloves **fresh garlic, grated**
1 **medium onion, chopped**
$1/8$ **green or red pepper, chopped**
pinch **of cilantro**
pinch **of oregano**
black or white pepper to taste
1 package **Sazon (with cilantro and achiote;**
   found at any Hispanic store)
6 **very green plantains**
2 $1/6$ oz. ($1/3$ of an 8-oz. can) **of tomato sauce**
salt to taste

Boil pork in salted water until very soft.

In a small frying pan, fry garlic, onion, peppers, cilantro, oregano, pepper and Sazon to make Sofrito, cooking on medium heat until onions are soft but not burnt.

Grate plantains. Add Sofrito, plantains and tomato sauce to boiling pork. Should be served as soon as it thickens. Don't let it stick to the pot. Add more water if needed. Salt to taste. Use low to medium heat until plantains are done and the soup is creamy. Serve with French bread.

Yields 6 small bowls of soup.

MARY'S PEANUT BUTTER CREAM PIE

Mary Carey
Mary's McKinley View Lodge
Mile A 134.5 Parks Highway

3/4 cup **granulated sugar**
1/4 cup **cornstarch**
1/2 tsp. **salt**
2 **eggs**
2 Tbs. **margarine or butter**
3 cups **milk**
1 Tbs. **vanilla**
4 rounded Tbs. **peanut butter**
1 **pie shell, baked**
whipped cream to taste

In the top of a double boiler, mix sugar, cornstarch and salt, then add slightly beaten eggs, butter or margarine, milk and vanilla. Cook over boiling water, whipping constantly with wire whisk, until it thickens. Mix in peanut butter, then pour into pie shell and let cool. Top with whipped cream before serving.

Serves 6 to 8.

On a clear day, Mary Carey's lodge presents an incomparable view of "her" mountain, which she happily shares with many visitors. Longtime homesteader, teacher, journalist and author, Mary thoroughly enjoys her role as a one-woman welcoming committee and limitless source of Alaska knowledge, assisted by her daughter, teacher and writer Jean Richardson.

PERCH CRACKED WHOLE WHEAT BREAD

Leslie LeQuire
The Perch
Mile A 224 Parks Highway

1 cup **warm water**
$1/4$ cup **oil**
2 packages **yeast**
2 cups **white flour**

$1/2$ cup **whole wheat flour**
$1/2$ cup **cracked wheat flour**
$1/4$ cup **granulated sugar**
$1/2$ tsp. **salt**

* NOTE: "Bread in a Bag" (available at The Perch) can
  substitute for all dry ingredients.

Pour water, oil and yeast into a large (4-qt.) mixing bowl. When yeast is dissolved, add all dry ingredients or contents of "Bread in a Bag."

Mix thoroughly or knead until very smooth. You may need to add a bit more white flour–do so only a tablespoon at a time. Dough should be soft and a bit sticky. Let rise about 1 hour, then place in a 9" X 5" pan. Let rise 30 minutes. Bake at 350°F for about 45 minutes.

For almost 10 years, Leslie LeQuire has owned and managed a gourmet's delight, The Perch, high on a hilltop just east of the Parks Highway at Milepost A 224. A loaf of her special bread accompanies every dinner at this scenic restaurant, rated by Frommer's travel guide as one of Alaska's 10 best places to dine. Other variety breads, as well as many types of pizza, are sold in the bakery/deli beside the highway. Lodging is available in rustic cabins throughout the surrounding woodlands.

Denali National Park

Denali National Park and Preserve was established in 1917 as Mount McKinley National Park. It was renamed Denali and designated a park and preserve by the Alaska National Interest Lands Conservation Act of 1980, which also enlarged the park to its present 6 million acres. The crown jewel of the park is Mount McKinley, also called Denali, at 20,320 feet, North America's highest mountain.

"Denali Lodging operates the Grande Denali Lodge and the Denali Bluffs Hotel. Located at Mile 238. 2 on the Parks Highway, the lodge and hotel are just one mile from the Denali National Park entrance. Both our hotels offer stunning views of the Alaska Range at both of our full-service restaurants."

HICKORY SMOKED PORK CHOP WITH APPLE CRANBERRY CONFIT

Jeffrey V. Bane, Executive Chef
Grande Denali Lodge & Resort
Denali Bluffs Hotel
Mile A 238.2 Parks Highway
Denali National Park, AK

4 (8 to 10 oz.) hickory smoked, bone-in pork chops
  (from your local butcher or meat counter)
1 cup spiced rum, heated
6 oz. dried cranberries
2 strips bacon, diced small
3 oz. shallots, diced small
3 Granny Smith apples, diced (hold in cold water)
1 Tbs. brown sugar
1 tsp. cider vinegar
1/4 cup chicken broth, heated
salt and pepper to season
2 tsp. cornstarch slurry (1 tsp. water mixed with
  1 tsp. cornstarch)

Preheat oven to 350°F with a shelf near the middle. Preheat grill on high heat. Quickly mark the pork chops off on the hot grill (creates grill marks on meat).

Place uncovered in an oven-safe pan. When sauce is about 15 minutes from being done, place pork chops in oven to finish.

Heat rum in microwave, then add cranberries, cover tightly and let sit for 10 minutes. Drain berries, reserving rum for later.

Heat a medium-sized saucepan over low heat. Add bacon and allow fat to render. Don't allow bacon to scorch. You may substitute oil for the bacon if you prefer. Add shallots and apples to saucepan and cook for 3 to 4 minutes on low heat until shallots soften and apples are about half-cooked. Next, add half of the rum you used for the cranberries and turn the heat up a bit to allow the rum to reduce by about half. If you are using a gas range, you can flame the mixture by allowing the pan to tilt just enough to allow flames to curl into the pan and ignite.

Add rum-soaked cranberries, brown sugar and vinegar. Add chicken broth and simmer for 5 minutes until all flavors meld. Adjust seasoning with salt and white pepper. Add cornstarch slurry one teaspoon at a time to give confit a nice shine and consistency. Confit should be thick and chunky.

When pork chops are ready, divide confit 4 ways and serve over the meat.

Suggested side dishes are roasted root vegetables, such as carrots, parsnips, onions and seasoned mashed potatoes or baked sweet potatoes.

Serves 4.

SALMON NUT LOG

Carol Crofoot
Overlook Bar & Grill at
Denali Crow's Nest Log Cabins
Mile A 238.5 Parks Highway
Denali National Park, AK

1 1/2 lbs. **fresh salmon**
3 lbs. **cream cheese**
3 bunches **green onions, finely chopped**
1/8 oz. **ground white pepper**
1/8 oz. **ground thyme**
1/4 fluid oz. **woodsmoke flavoring**
pecans or walnuts, chopped to coat
parsley, chopped to coat

Cook salmon in microwave. Soften cream cheese and mix
with salmon, onions, pepper, thyme and woodsmoke
flavoring until just combined. Roll in nuts and parsley to
lightly coat outside. Serve with crackers of your choice.
Store in plastic wrap and chill or freeze.

Serves 12.

SASHI'S DAHL SOUP

Carol Crofoot
Overlook Bar & Grill at
Denali Crow's Nest Log Cabins
Mile A 238.5 Parks Highway
Denali National Park, AK

"A hot, spicy Indian yellow split pea soup."

1 cup **dahl (yellow split peas), washed**
5 $1/2$ cups **cold water**
1 Tbs. **salt**
1 $1/2$ tsp. **haldi (turmeric)**
6 cloves **garlic**
1 Tbs. **fresh cilantro, chopped**
1 **habeñero chili, seeds removed**
$1/4$ cup **oil (preferably mustard oil, but soy oil will work)**
$1/4$ tsp. **cumin seeds, not powdered**
$1/2$ **large onion, finely chopped**

Mix water, salt and haldi and add to dahl. Bring to boil and simmer, covered, for 1 hour. Smash together garlic, cilantro and habeñero and set aside.

In a separate pan, heat oil over high heat. Add cumin seeds when oil is hot, then add onion. Sauté about 4 minutes until onion is just barely browned. Add garlic mixture and sauté about 1 $1/2$ additional minutes. Add several large spoonfuls of dahl and water mixture, stirring often. Pour this mixture back into the split peas and heat to serve.

Serves 8 to 10.

COCONUT OATMEAL COOKIES

Laura Cole, from *A Cache of Recipes*
Camp Denali and North Face Lodge
Denali National Park, AK

"Chip coconut gives these cookies wonderful texture and a unique appearance. Chip coconut is large-flake, unsweetened coconut and can be found in bulk at many health food stores. If you have difficulty locating it, substitute with shredded unsweetened coconut. The cookies won't look as unique, but they'll still taste great."

3 cups **all-purpose flour**
1 1/2 tsp. **baking powder**
1 1/2 tsp. **baking soda**
1/2 tsp. **salt**
3/8 lb. (1 1/2 sticks) **butter, softened**
1 1/4 cups **brown sugar**

1/2 cup **granulated sugar**
2 **eggs**
1 Tbs. **vanilla extract**
1 1/4 cups **rolled oats**
2 1/4 cups **chip coconut**

Preheat oven to 350°F. In a large bowl, combine flour, baking powder, baking soda and salt. In a seperate large bowl, using an electric mixer fitted with paddle attachment, beat together butter and sugars, beating until light and fluffy. Add eggs one at a time, then add vanilla. Beat until light and fluffy. Slowly incorporate flour mixture until well combined. Mix in oats and coconut.

Using a tablespoon, scoop out spoonfuls of dough onto baking sheets lined with parchment paper. Bake for 8 to 10 minutes. Cool on pans or cooling racks. Store in an airtight container.

Yields 3 dozen cookies.

GRANOLA

Laura Cole, from *A Cache of Recipes*
Camp Denali and North Face Lodge
Denali National Park, AK

"Homemade granola is such a satisfying treat. A mouthwatering aroma fills the kitchen as it bakes. This always makes a great gift, and you can customize it by adding dried fruits of your choice."

$1/2$ cup **vegetable oil**
1 cup **honey**
1 Tbs. **vanilla extract**
2 tsp. **almond extract**
2 Tbs. **water**
7 cups **rolled oats**
2 cups **wheat germ**

2 cups **flaked coconut**
$2/3$ cup **sesame seeds**
$1/2$ cup **sunflower seeds**
$1/2$ cup **bran flakes**
1 cup **nuts (such as almonds, pecans or hazelnuts), coarsely chopped**

Preheat oven to 275°F. Lightly grease shallow roasting pan. In a small saucepan over medium heat, combine oil, honey, vanilla and almond extracts and water. Heat until well combined and set aside. In a large bowl, mix together oats, wheat germ, coconut, sesame seeds, sunflower seeds, bran flakes and nuts. Pour honey mixture over dry ingredients. Mix well to thoroughly combine; mixing with your hands works best. Transfer to prepared roasting pan. Bake, uncovered, for about 90 minutes, stirring every 15 minutes to prevent burning. Bake until completely dry and golden brown. Allow to cool completely. Store in an airtight container.

Yields 14 cups.

DILL RYE BREAD

Laura Cole, from *A Cache of Recipes*
Camp Denali and North Face Lodge
Denali National Park, AK

"This bread tastes especially wonderful when served with smoked Alaskan halibut or salmon."

1 1/2 cups **warm water**
1 cup **sourdough starter** *(next page)*
2 Tbs. **honey**
2 Tbs. **molasses**
1 Tbs. **active dry yeast**
1/4 cup **pure gluten flour**
1 1/2 cups **rye flour**

4 1/2 cups **all-purpose flour**
2 Tbs. **dried onion**
1 Tbs. **dried dill weed**
1 tsp. **dill seeds**
1 Tbs. **salt**
1/4 cup **olive oil**
1 Tbs. **butter, melted**

In the bowl of an electric mixer, combine water, sourdough starter, honey and molasses. Using a rubber spatula, mix in yeast. Allow yeast to dissolve and become frothy. In a separate bowl, combine flours, onion, dill weed, dill seeds and salt. With a rubber spatula, mix half of the flour mixture into the yeast mixture. Using the dough hook attachment on mixer, slowly incorporate the remaining flour mixture, alternating with olive oil. Continue to add flour until dough is smooth, soft and elastic.

Turn dough out into an oiled bowl, turning it to oil the top. Cover loosely and let rise in a warm place until almost doubled in volume. Gently punch down the dough, and turn out onto a lightly floured surface. Divide the dough in half. Knead and shape dough into oblong loaves. Place on a lightly buttered sheet pan. Cover loosely, and let rise in a warm place until almost doubled in volume.

Preheat oven to 375°F. Brush tops of loaves with melted butter. Gently slash tops of loaves diagonally, making 3 cuts, 1/4" deep, per loaf. Bake at 375°F for 20 minutes. Reduce heat to 325°F, and continue to bake for an additional 20 to 25 minutes. Remove from oven, and remove from the pan. Cool completely on a cooling rack before slicing.

Yields 2 1-lb. loaves.

Sourdough Starter:

"Original starters may have owed their particular flavor to wild yeasts captured from the air when a mixture of flour and water was allowed to ferment over a couple of days. Here is the recipe for a speedier version."

2 cups **warm water**
1 Tbs. **active dry yeast**
2 cups **all-purpose flour**

In a bowl, measure the warm water, add the yeast and allow to dissolve. Mix in flour, a little at a time. When well mixed, transfer starter to a ceramic crock. Loosely cover (a plate will do.). Allow starter to rest at room temperature for 48 hours prior to use.

To replenish starter, add equal parts water and flour. Once you have the starter, you can keep it going indefinitely. You can store your starter in the refrigerator; just allow it to come to room temperature before using. If any liquid rises to the top, stir it back in.

Yields 2 cups starter.

RUSTIC NECTARINE AND PLUM GALETTE

Laura Cole, from *A Cache of Recipes*
Camp Denali and North Face Lodge
Denali National Park, AK

"Cream cheese in the tart dough gives it a very delicate crumb and at the same time makes it a bit easier to work with than an all-butter tart dough."

Tart Shell:
1/2 cup **granulated sugar**
5 Tbs. **butter, softened**
1/2 tsp. **vanilla extract**
2 Tbs. (1 oz.) **cream cheese**
1 **egg**
2 cups **all-purpose flour**
1/4 tsp. **salt**

Filling:
5 **plums, halved and pitted, each half cut into 6 slices**
5 **nectarines, halved and pitted, each half cut into 6 slices**
1/2 tsp. **ground ginger**
6 Tbs. **granulated sugar, divided**
1 Tbs. **all-purpose flour**
2 Tbs. **butter, melted**
1 **egg, whisked to blend**
1/4 cup **apricot preserves**

For tart shell: Using an electric mixer fitted with the paddle attachment, mix together sugar, butter, vanilla and cream cheese until light and fluffy. Slowly incorporate egg. On low speed, quickly add flour and salt. Mix just until dough forms. Gather dough into a ball and gently press into a disk. Wrap in plastic wrap and freeze for 1 hour.

For filling: Preheat oven to 400°F. In a large bowl, toss together plums, nectarines, ginger and 4 Tbs. of sugar.

To assemble and bake tart: Remove dough from freezer. On a lightly floured surface, roll dough into a 14" round. Transfer to a sheet pan lined with parchment paper. Mix 1 Tbs. of remaining sugar with flour and sprinkle over dough, leaving a 2" border at the edge. Leaving the border plain, arrange the nectarines and plums in alternating concentric circles, working from the outside toward the center. Drizzle the melted butter over the fruit. Fold the dough border in toward the center of the tart. Brush the exterior of the border with the whisked egg and sprinkle with the remaining 1 Tbs. sugar. Bake until fruit is tender and crust is golden brown, about 45 minutes.

In a small saucepan over low heat, melt apricot preserves until thin and brush over top of tart. Allow tart to cool on sheet pan for 1 hour. Run a long, thin knife under tart to loosen it. Carefully transfer it to a serving platter, or cut it into the desired portions and serve from the pan.

Yields 1 10" galette. Serves 10.

SPINACH SALAD WITH ROASTED PEARS AND SUGARED PECANS

Laura Cole, from *A Cache of Recipes*
Camp Denali and North Face Lodge
Denali National Park, AK

"Although pears are available year-round, this salad is best in early autumn, when pears are at their flavor peak. To make this salad a main course, add Roquefort cheese. The salty richness of the cheese pairs well with the sweetness of the pears."

3 **ripe Bartlett pears**
1 **lb. bunch baby spinach leaves with stems removed**
1 Tbs. **shallots, minced**
2 Tbs. **champagne vinegar**
2 Tbs. **apple cider**
1 Tbs. **honey**
1 Tbs. **honey mustard**
1 tsp. **kosher salt**
1 tsp. **pepper, freshly ground**
1 cup **olive oil**
1 cup **sugared pecans** *(recipe follows)*

Preheat oven to 375°F. Wash, core and slice each of the pears into 12 sections. Set pear slices on a baking sheet. Roast for 10 to 12 minutes, removing them from the oven when they are just beginning to color. Set aside to cool.

Wash and spin dry the spinach leaves. In a large bowl, combine the shallots, vinegar, cider, honey, mustard, salt and pepper. Slowly whisk in the olive oil.

Gently toss the spinach with dressing to coat. Arrange pears on the desired number of plates. Top with dressed spinach and garnish with sugared pecans.

Serves 8.

Sugared Pecans:

"These are great as a salad garnish or on their own as a snack."

2 cups **pecan halves**
2 Tbs. **honey**
2 Tbs. **vegetable oil**
2 Tbs. **water**
1/2 cup **granulated sugar**
1 Tbs. **kosher salt**
1/2 tsp. **cayenne pepper**

Preheat oven to 375°F. Spread pecan halves on rimmed baking sheet. Toast for 10 to 12 minutes. Pecans should be very fragrant. Remove from oven and set aside to cool.

In a small saucepan over medium heat, combine honey, oil and water. Bring to a boil, reduce heat and add pecans. Stir together until all liquid is absorbed. In a separate bowl, combine sugar, salt and cayenne pepper. Mix in pecans, stirring to coat. Spread out sugared pecans on parchment paper and allow to cool completely. Store in airtight container. Use 1 cup as a garnish for Spinach Salad with Roasted Pears.

Yields 2 cups.

SOUTHWESTERN KIPPERED SALMON SALAD

Laura Cole, from *A Cache of Recipes*
Camp Denali and North Face Lodge
Denali National Park, AK

"This salad has quite a kick to it. If you prefer a milder dish, omit the adobo sauce. Try serving it wrapped in a tortilla for a quick sandwich on the go. Adobo sauce can be found in the Mexican foods section of most supermarkets. You can freeze any sauce you have left over, or store it in the refrigerator. It will keep for a few weeks."

1 cup **sour cream**
1 tsp. **adobo sauce**
2 cups **flaked kippered salmon**
$1/2$ cup **cucumber, peeled, seeded and diced**
$1/4$ cup **red bell pepper, diced**
$1/4$ cup **red onion, minced**
$1/3$ cup **fresh cilantro, chopped**
2 tsp. **chili powder**
2 tsp. **ground cumin**
salt to taste

In a small bowl, combine sour cream and adobo sauce and set aside. In a large bowl, combine salmon, cucumber, red pepper, onion, cilantro, chili powder, cumin and salt. Mix well and add sour cream mixture. Taste, and adjust seasonings. Serve immediately.

Yields 4 cups.

Fairbanks

Fairbanks, founded in the early years of the 20th century, is Alaska's "Golden Heart City." Although retaining the spirit of its rich history, this city of approximately 30,000 offers all features and amenities of a modern community. This is the service and supply center for the vast Interior, as well as for the North Slope's extensive industrial activities, in which the city played a key role during construction of the trans-Alaska pipeline in the 1970s. Government and military entities account for about half of the area's employment, with extractive industries such as oil and mining continuing major roles in the area's economy. Tourism has become a rapidly growing industry because of the appeal of the Interior and its hospitable "golden heart" in Fairbanks.

MINI CRAB QUICHE

Jeanne Long
A-1 Yankovich Inn B&B
Fairbanks, AK

"These are a couple of recipes that have been in the family for a long time."

1 tube **large refrigerated buttermilk biscuits**
1 can (8 oz.) **cleaned and flaked crabmeat**
  (or 1 cup imitation crabmeat, chopped)
$1/2$ cup **Swiss cheese, shredded**
$1/2$ cup **milk**
1 **egg**
$1/2$ tsp. **dill weed**
$1/4$ tsp. **salt**

Separate biscuits until you have 12 pieces. Press each piece into the bottom and up the sides of a muffin pan. Divide crab equally among the 12 quiches (about 2 tsp. a piece), then add about 1 tsp. Swiss cheese to each. In a small bowl, combine milk, egg, dill weed and salt. Put about 2 to 3 tsp. of this mixture into each quiche. Bake at 375°F for about 30 minutes until edges of dough are golden brown. Let stand for 5 minutes before removing from pans.

Serve with crisp bacon and fruit.

Yields 12.

RHUBARB CUSTARD PIE

Jeanne Long
A-1 Yankovich Inn B&B
Fairbanks, AK

"One time, I had some people here from Scottsdale, Arizona. One of the guests, upon finding the rhubarb in my garden, asked me if I could bake a really good rhubarb pie. I told him I could and asked if he wanted a slice in the afternoon. He wanted it at breakfast time. So breakfast came around, and there were other people in the B&B at the time, so after the regular breakfast, they all had pie and coffee and had a wonderful time. They loved the pie, and they all took home this recipe."

"This recipe originally came from Sweden, my parents' homeland, and it goes back at least 3 generations that I know of. It has been in the family for a very long time."

Pie Crust:
3 cups **flour**
1 1/2 cups **shortening**
1 **egg**
1 Tbs. **vinegar**
1/3 cup **water**

Rhubarb Filling:
1 cup plus 1/2 tsp. **granulated sugar**
1 1/2 cups **rhubarb, cut into 1" pieces**
2 **eggs**
1 Tbs. **cornstarch**
1 tsp. **flour**

For pie crust: Mix pie crust ingredients together. Knead dough. Dividing equally, roll out 1 piece to line an 8" pie pan and reserve second piece for top.

For filling: Mix together rhubarb filling ingredients and pour into prepared crust. Roll out reserved dough; cut and weave a lattice top crust. Sprinkle top of pie with about 1/2 tsp. sugar.

Bake at 350°F for about 1 hour. To test if custard is done, use a knife to see if any filling clings. If it does, bake a little longer.

BILLIE'S BREAD

Billie Cook, Billie's Backpackers Hostel
Fairbanks, AK

"I serve this bread to my hostelers about 2 times a week. One Japanese guest was a composer and wrote a melody called 'Billie's Bread.' It's a lovely peppy tune in honor of a loaf of bread I perfected while I was in Galena, AK, as a bride, back in the 1960s. This bread has served us well!"

4 cups **warm water**
2 Tbs. **salt**
1 Tbs. **Crisco® shortening or oil**

$1/2$ cup **granulated sugar**
3 Tbs. **yeast**
about 4 cups **flour**

In a large bowl, stir together all ingredients except flour until sugar and salt are dissolved. Add flour cup by cup, and stir until you can no longer stir with a spoon. (I keep adding flour and kneading right in the large bowl.) Add flour to bottom of bowl and knead dough until stiff. (To test, poke your finger in the top of the dough. If it doesn't leave much of an indent, and dough feels velvety, it's ready to rise.) Leave dough in bowl. Cover with clean, white, damp cloth, and place in a draft-free place (your microwave may be a good place). Let rise until doubled in size.

Knead dough again, divide and place in 3 loaf pans. Preheat oven to 400°F. Then, turn heat down to 350°F. When bread has again doubled in size, bake for 1 hour. (Sometimes, I completely cover the top of the loaf with Parmesan cheese before baking. Loaves may also be coated with egg white before baking.) To test if bread is done, knock on the top of the loaf; if it sounds hollow, it's done. If the top is done before the hour is up, cover the loaf with tin foil and continue baking.

Yields 3 loaves.

BREAKFAST CASSEROLE

Barbara Neubauer
Fairbanks Bed & Breakfast
Fairbanks, AK

2 lbs. **sausage (tube variety)**
1 2-lb. bag **of Ore Ida® (or O'Brian's®) Breakfast Potatoes**
16 oz. **sour cream**
1 10.5-oz. can **cream of potato, mushroom or celery soup**
10.5 oz. (1 soup can full) **milk**
salt and pepper to taste
2 cups **cheddar cheese, shredded**
1 cup **onion, chopped**

Preheat oven to 400°F. Brown sausage and drain grease. Mix thawed potatoes, sour cream, soup, onions, milk and sausage in bowl. Add salt and pepper to taste. Pour into casserole dish and evenly cover with shredded cheese. Bake for 45 minutes to 1 hour.

This recipe can be made a day early and reheated.

Serves 10 to 12.

PEACH CRISP

Barbara Neubauer
Fairbanks Bed & Breakfast
Fairbanks, AK

"I have used this as a dessert or coffee cake for mornings. This dish is good hot or cold."

1 large can (29 oz.) **sliced peaches and juice**
1 box **yellow cake mix**
$1/2$ cup **butter, melted (do not substitute)**
1 cup **shredded coconut**
1 cup **pecans, chopped**

Spread peaches and juice evenly in an ungreased 9" X 13" dish. Break up or sift cake mix to remove lumps, then spread over peaches. Drizzle butter over top of cake mix. Sprinkle coconut and pecans on top. Bake at 375°F for 55 minutes.

Serves 12.

SAUSAGE BRUNCH

Barbara Neubauer
Fairbanks Bed & Breakfast
Fairbanks, AK

2 1/2 cups **seasoned herb croutons**
2 cups **sharp cheddar cheese, shredded**
1 1/2 lbs. **link sausage**
4 **eggs**
1 3/4 cups **milk**
3/4 tsp. **dry mustard**
1/2 tsp. **salt**
dash **of pepper**
1 can (10.5 oz.) **cream of mushroom soup (or any creamed soup)**

Place croutons on bottom of greased 8" X 12" pan. Top with
1 1/2 cups cheese; save 1/2 cup for top. Brown and drain
sausage, cut into pieces and place on top of croutons and
cheese. Beat eggs with 1 1/4 cups milk and seasonings. Pour
over casserole. Refrigerate overnight. The next day, dilute
mushroom soup with 1/2 cup milk and pour over casserole.
Sprinkle with remaining cheese. Bake at 300°F for 1 hour.

Serves 8 to 10.

CAPPUCCINO CHIP MUFFINS
Leicha Welton, 7 Gables Inn & Suites
Fairbanks, AK

2 cups **all-purpose flour**
3/4 cup **granulated sugar**
1 Tbs. **baking powder**
2 tsp. **instant espresso coffee powder**
1/2 tsp. **salt**
1/2 tsp. **ground cinnamon**

1 cup **milk**
1/2 cup **butter, melted**
1 **egg, lightly beaten**
1 tsp. **vanilla**
3/4 cup **semisweet chocolate mini-chips**

Preheat oven to 350°F. Grease large muffin tin.

In large bowl, stir together flour, sugar, baking powder, espresso powder, salt and cinnamon. In separate bowl, stir together milk, butter, egg and vanilla until blended. Add milk mixture to dry ingredients and stir to combine. Mix in chocolate chips.

Spoon batter into prepared muffin cups. Bake 20 minutes or until top springs back when lightly touched. Remove muffins from pan and cool on wire rack. Serve with Chocolate Cream Cheese Espresso Spread *(recipe follows)*.

Chocolate Cream Cheese Espresso Spread:

4 oz. **cream cheese, softened**
1 square (1 oz.) **semisweet chocolate, melted**

1 Tbs. **granulated sugar**
1/2 tsp. **vanilla**
1/2 tsp. **instant espresso powder**

Blend all ingredients together thoroughly in a small bowl. Serve as frosting for Cappuccino Chip Muffins.

Yields 12 large frosted muffins.

LEMON SQUARES

Leicha Welton
7 Gables Inn & Suites
Fairbanks, AK

1 cup **butter**
$1/2$ cup **confectioner's sugar**
2 $1/3$ cups **flour**
4 **eggs**
2 cups **granulated sugar**
$1/3$ cup **frozen lemonade concentrate**
1 tsp. **baking powder**

Cream butter and confectioner's sugar. Add 2 cups flour, and blend together. Spread evenly into greased 9" X 13" baking pan. Bake at 350°F for 20 minutes.

Beat eggs until light and foamy. Gradually add granulated sugar. Add lemonade concentrate, remaining $1/3$ cup flour and baking powder. Beat thoroughly. Pour mixture over baked crust. Bake an additional 25 to 30 minutes. Cut into 1" squares. Sprinkle with additional confectioner's sugar for garnish.

Yields approximately 36 squares.

STAR SAUSAGE WON TONS

Leicha Welton
7 Gables Inn & Suites
Fairbanks, AK

2 cups (1 lb.) **cooked sausage, crumbled**
1 1/2 cups **cheddar cheese, grated**
1 1/2 cups **Monterey Jack cheese, grated**
1/2 cup **dry ranch salad dressing mix**
1 can (4.25 oz.) **chopped ripe olives**
1/2 cup **crushed red pepper**
1 package **won ton wrappers**

Preheat oven to 350°F.

Combine sausage, cheeses, salad dressing mix, olives and red pepper in large bowl. Lightly grease a standard-sized muffin tin, and press one won ton wrapper in each cup. Brush with oil. Bake 5 minutes or until golden. Remove from tins and place on baking sheet. Fill each won ton 3/4 full with sausage mixture. Return to oven for 5 minutes or until bubbly.

Yields 4 to 5 dozen.

QUICK ROLLS
Patricia Jones, Beaver Point Lodge
60 miles west of Fairbanks, AK

1/2 cup **milk**
1 cup **water**
1/4 cup **butter**
4 cups **all-purpose flour**

2 Tbs. **granulated sugar**
1 tsp. **salt**
2 envelopes **quick-rising yeast**
butter or margarine to grease pan

On low heat, warm milk with water and melt butter into the mixture. Keep fluids only moderately warm, from 120°F to 130°F (or heat until slightly more than warm to the touch, not hot). Mix together 1 1/2 cups flour, sugar, salt and yeast and add liquid mixture. Stir rapidly for 2 minutes. Add about 1/2 cup additional flour and stir again for another 2 minutes. Add about 2 cups additional flour and stir just until ball forms. Turn out onto floured board and knead for 10 minutes, adding flour as needed.

Place dough in a pan, greased with butter or margarine, and cover with a damp dish towel. Set covered pan in a warm place. (I set it on top of a pan of water on top of our wood-stove.) Let dough rest for 10 to 15 minutes. Turn dough out onto board and, using a serrated knife, cut into equal parts.

For regular-sized dinner rolls, cut dough into 24 equal parts and roll each into a uniformly shaped ball. Divide in half and place in 2 generously greased 9" round cake pans. Cover pans with damp dish towel and set in warm place to rise again for 60 to 90 minutes. Bake at 350°F for about 15 minutes. Turn pans upside-down on dinner plate and gently tap rolls out. The round of rolls will hold together nicely for serving.

BEAVER POINT'S BEEF BARLEY STEW

Patricia Jones, Beaver Point Lodge
60 miles west of Fairbanks, AK

"This hearty stew can simmer over a woodstove, which is what we use for heat here at our remote lodge. Typically, I'll put together the stew and let it slow cook on the stove in the afternoon hours, creating a wonderful aroma to enjoy when folks come in from enjoying outdoor activities. Usually, I serve this with homemade rolls.

"Moose can be substituted for beef. If so, I recommend a marinade to add moisture and to tenderize."

2 to 3 lbs. **beef stew meat**
2 Tbs. **oil**
Mrs. Dash® Salt-free seasoning to taste
3 cubes **beef bouillon**
3 cups **boiling water**
2 cloves **fresh garlic, sliced**
butter to sauté garlic
8 to 10 fresh **mushrooms, sliced, or** 1 4-oz. can **mushrooms, including liquid**
1 cup **baby carrots, sliced**
1/4 cup **onions, minced**
1 Tbs. **Worcestershire sauce**
1/4 cup **red cooking wine**
fresh ground pepper
1 cup **pearl barley (can also use quick barley)**
2 1/2 cups **water**
additional liquid as needed

Trim stew meat and cut into bite-sized pieces. Marinate for 30 minutes, if desired, to tenderize and add flavor.

Heat oil in a skillet and brown meat quickly to seal in moisture, seasoning with Mrs. Dash. Place in an 8-quart stockpot.

Dissolve bouillon in 3 cups boiling water and add to meat. Sauté garlic in butter and add to meat with mushrooms, carrots, onion, Worcestershire sauce, wine and pepper. Partially cook pearl barley in 2 1/2 cups water and add to stew. (If using quick barley, do not cook before adding to stew.) Simmer until barley completely puffs and carrots have softened, a minimum of 2 hours. Add additional liquid as needed.

Serves 6 to 8.

"Nestled in the forested Dugan Hills on the shore of a remote lake, Beaver Point Lodge is located about 60 miles west of Fairbanks, Alaska. Access in summer is by floatplane and in winter by ski or wheeled aircraft or by snow machines or dog teams. The historic Fairbanks-to-Manley Hot Springs mail trail cuts through the wilderness surrounding our 540-acre, arrowhead-shaped lake, home to a wide range of wildlife and waterfowl.

"Guests at this family-run lodge enjoy a full slate of summer and winter activities, as they experience a simple but comfortable rural lifestyle, assisted in many ways by modern technology.

"Guests share meals and conversations in our main facility while enjoying the calm quietness of a private log cabin overlooking the lake. (Groups are welcomed year-round.)

"We enjoy sharing our rural lifestyle with people who appreciate Alaska's wilderness and the peaceful atmosphere it can provide."

PATRICIA'S CHOCOLATE RASPBERRY DREAM DESSERT

Patricia Jones, Beaver Point Lodge
60 miles west of Fairbanks, AK

"I modified this family dessert recipe last winter, then when wild raspberries became available during summer, modified it again. I made it for my niece's Bat Mitzvah last winter, and it was a big hit, even among the multitude of desserts and cookies at the afternoon luncheon.

"We usually serve this dessert after the evening meal at our lodge. Although this spring, we hosted six trailbreakers working on the altered race route of the Iditarod Trail Sled Dog Race, and they were too full from dinner to really enjoy dessert."

2 cups **fresh raspberries**
$1/2$ cup **granulated sugar**
1 package **white cake mix**
1 $1/4$ cups **oatmeal, uncooked**
8 Tbs. **butter, softened**
1 **egg**
$1/4$ cup **brown sugar**
$1/4$ cup **pecans, chopped (optional)**
1 cup **chocolate chips**

Mix raspberries with sugar. Set aside for 1 hour or more. Mix together cake mix, 1 cup of the oatmeal and 6 Tbs. of the butter until crumbly. Reserve 1 cup of crumb mixture. Add egg, slightly beaten, to remaining crumb mixture. This will make a slightly sticky crumbly mixture. Press into well-greased 9" X 13" baking dish. Bake at 350°F for about 5 to 10 minutes.

To the reserved cup of crumb mixture, add 2 Tbs. butter, 1/4 cup oatmeal, brown sugar and pecans. Cut into a crumbly mixture and set aside. Remove bottom crust from oven and spread raspberry mixture over top. Sprinkle chocolate chips over raspberry mixture and top with final crumb mixture. Bake at 350°F for an additional 20 to 30 minutes until lightly browned. Let set for a few minutes before serving. This dessert is great with vanilla ice cream.

Serves 8 to 10.

"Meals at Beaver Point Lodge are served family-style and are highlighted by homemade breads and desserts. Many dishes served at our facility have evolved from our Midwestern roots, spiced by an Alaska flavor. Since opening for business, word has spread among local aviators that our lakeside dock, coffeepot and cookie jar stand ready and welcome for aircraft drop-ins."

TWO RIVERS BOUILLABAISSE WITH ROUILLE

Anthony Marsico, Chef
Two Rivers Lodge
Mile J 16 Chena Hot Springs Road

"A world-class recipe for bouillabaisse which is accompanied by a garlic and saffron paste known as Rouille. The Rouille is spooned into each serving to individual taste."

1/2 cup **white wine**
2 cups **fish stock (or clam juice)**
2 **Italian plum tomatoes, pureed**
4 cloves **garlic, mashed**
1 **small onion, diced**
1 **bay leaf**
1/4 **green pepper, diced**
1/2 **stalk celery, diced**
1 tsp. **red pepper flakes**
1/2 tsp. **cayenne pepper**
dash **of salt**
freshly ground black pepper to taste
pinch **of saffron**
4 **large prawns, shell on or off**
2 **king crab claws, cracked**
1 8-oz. **fish filet (snapper, redfish, salmon), cut in half**
4 **large sea scallops**
2 **oysters on the half shell (shells washed)**
8 **steamer clams, rinsed**
8 **mussels, rinsed**
1 **soft-shell crab, cut in half**
2 **slipper lobster tails (or other lobster)**

Combine wine, fish stock, garlic and all ingredients except seafood in a saucepan. Bring broth to a rolling boil for 5 minutes. Reduce temperature to medium-low. Drop in fish filets, scallops, clams and mussels. Let simmer 2 minutes, then drop in remaining ingredients. Increase temperature. When soup comes to a rolling boil, turn off heat. Check clams to see if they are open. Ladle into a tureen and serve 2 to 4 people, with each person spooning Rouille *(recipe follows)* into their soup and allowing it to steep. Or spread Rouille on slices of French bread, and place in each bowl.

Rouille:
$^1/4$ cup **clam nectar**
$^1/2$ cup **bread cubes**
8 cloves **garlic, mashed**
2 tsp. **olive oil**
$^1/4$ tsp. **saffron threads**

Soak bread in clam juice for 5 minutes. Stir in remaining ingredients and mix thoroughly. Allow to sit $^1/2$ hour to overnight.

Serves 2 to 4.

ALMOND DATE BREAD

Bryan Hanson, Chef
Chena Hot Springs Resort
Mile J 56.6 Chena Hot Springs Road

2 Tbs. **active dry yeast**
2 1/2 cups **water**
6 cups **all-purpose flour**
1 Tbs. **salt**
1 cup **almonds, sliced**
1 cup **dates, chopped**
1/2 cup **olive oil**
2 **egg whites, whisked for glaze**

Activate yeast with one cup of warm water. Set aside to "bloom" for 10 minutes. Add yeast and water to mixing bowl or electric mixer. Add remaining water, flour, salt, dates, nuts and olive oil to yeast and water. Mix with bread hook or wooden spoon for 8 to 10 minutes until dough comes away from the bowl; the mixture should be moist, satiny and a little sticky. Place the dough in a greased bowl covered with a clean dish towel. Let rise in a warm place until double in size, 1 to 2 hours.

Divide the dough into 3 portions, and shape the dough into balls. Place on parchment-paper-lined sheet tray; flatten dough to resemble round discs. Let rise another 1/2 hour. Gently brush with egg-white glaze. With a sharp knife, slash the top of the dough to make an "X." Bake at 450°F for 15 minutes. Then, lower oven temperature to 350°F and bake for 30 more minutes. Let cool 30 minutes before cutting.

Yields 3 loaves

FETA DIP

Bryan Hanson, Chef
Chena Hot Springs Resort
Mile J 56.6 Chena Hot Springs Road

Use with raw vegetables or shellfish.

1 cup **sour cream**
3/4 cup **mayonnaise**
1 cup **feta cheese, finely crumbled**
1 Tbs. **Worcestershire sauce**
3/4 Tbs. **white wine vinegar**
1 Tbs. **garlic**
1/2 cup **chopped fresh parsley**
salt and pepper to taste

Combine all ingredients in mixing bowl. Adjust seasoning and consistency to taste.

Yields 2 cups.

CHENA SPINACH SALAD

Bryan Hanson
Chena Hot Springs Resort
Mile J 56.6 Chena Hot Springs Road

2 lbs. spinach, cleaned and trimmed
1 red onion, sliced very thin
1 cup roasted pecans, roughly chopped
1 cup smoked Gouda cheese, diced 1/2"
2 cups roasted shallot bacon vinaigrette *(recipe follows)*

Toss all ingredients together in a large mixing bowl, reserving some of the pecans and cheese for garnish. Portion salad mixture into large serving bowls or onto individual plates. Garnish with pecans and cheese.

Roasted Shallot Bacon Vinaigrette:

6 bacon slices, finely chopped
1 Tbs. rosemary
1 Tbs. garlic, finely chopped
1 cup apple cider vinegar

6 shallots peeled
1 cup olive oil
1 Tbs. Dijon mustard
salt and pepper to taste

Simmer bacon, rosemary, garlic and apple cider vinegar until bacon renders fat, about 15 minutes. Set aside to cool.

Toss shallots in a little olive oil and salt and pepper. Put in pan, cover with foil and roast at 400°F for 30 minutes or until soft.

Add all ingredients, except olive oil, into blender or food processor. Puree until smooth. Add olive oil in a slow, steady stream. Thin with a little apple cider vinegar if necessary. Serve either warm or cold.

Yields 2 cups.

Chena Hot Springs, named for the nearby Chena River, was first reported in 1904 by the U.S. Geological Survey, and it's been a popular year-round destination for Interior residents ever since, although Chena Hot Springs Road wasn't completed until the late 1960s. The drive out to Chena Hot Springs Resort, located some 60-odd miles from Fairbanks at the end of the road, passes through the rolling hills northeast of Fairbanks and into the scenic Chena River valley. The area is popular with fishermen, canoeists, campers and hikers. The year-round Chena Hot Springs Resort offers lodging and a dining room, along with spring-fed indoor and outdoor pools.

PASTA CON FUNGI

Bryan Hanson, Chef
Chena Hot Springs Resort
Mile J 56.6 Chena Hot Springs Road

"Rigatoni pasta tossed with a grilled portobello sauce."

4 large portobello mushrooms, whole, stemmed and
  gills trimmed off
1/2 cup olive oil
1 lb. rigatoni pasta
1 onion, julienned
1 zucchini, julienned
1 red bell pepper, julienned
1 cup white wine
2 Tbs. garlic, finely chopped
1 cup heavy cream

Brush mushrooms with olive oil and grill 5 to 10 minutes
until cooked through. Set aside to cool, then slice 1/2" thick.
Bring a gallon of salted water to boil in large pot; add
rigatoni and blanch 10 to 15 minutes until al dente.

Sauté until softened (3 to 4 minutes) over moderate heat in
remaining olive oil: onion, zucchini, bell pepper. Add sliced
mushrooms, wine and garlic and simmer 3 to 4 minutes.
Add cream and simmer 5 to 10 minutes until sauce is thick
and reduced.

Drain pasta, and add to pan with sauce. Toss thoroughly
and serve.

Can be garnished with fresh, grated parmesan cheese or
long slices of garlic bread.

Richardson Highway

The 366-mile-long Richardson Highway connects the port of Valdez on Prince William Sound with Fairbanks in Interior Alaska, closely paralleling the trans-Alaska pipeline for much of its length. The Richardson Highway was Alaska's first road, known to early gold seekers as the Valdez to Eagle Trail, and reminders of this past are found at highway interpretive sites along the way. A very scenic route, the Richardson Highway crosses both the Chugach and Alaska mountain ranges.

STRAWBERRY-RHUBARB PIE

Todd and Patty Denton
Sourdough Roadhouse
Mile V 147.7 Richardson Highway

1 qt. **rhubarb, chopped**
1/2 cup **granulated sugar**
1/2 cup **strawberry JELL-O® Brand Gelatin**
2 cups **frozen strawberries, whole**
1 9" **sourdough pie crust, unbaked**
   (see recipe on next page)
water
cinnamon sugar

Add rhubarb, sugar and JELL-O® to 2-quart saucepan. Bring to a boil, and shut off heat. Add frozen strawberries, and mix. Pour into unbaked pie crust. Top with second unbaked pie crust. Cut holes in top crust for vents. Spray with water, and sprinkle with cinnamon sugar. Place on baking sheet and bake at 400°F for about 45 minutes or until crust is brown.

Serves 8 to 10.

Sourdough Pie Crust

Todd and Patty Denton
Sourdough Roadhouse
Mile V 147.7 Richardson Highway

2 cups **flour**
1 tsp. **salt**
$^1/_2$ tsp. **baking soda**
$^2/_3$ cup **shortening**
$^2/_3$ cup **sourdough starter** *(recipe on page 107)*

Sift flour, salt and baking soda together. Cut in shortening. Add sourdough starter and knead until dough leaves side of bowl. Set aside, covered, and let rise about $^1/_2$ hour. Roll dough out, place in pie plate and fill with your choice of pie filling. Top with additional rolled-out crust. Bake at approximately 375°F until crust is brown.

Yields 1 double-crust pie. Serves about 6 to 8.

A hundred years ago, the original Sourdough Roadhouse opened along Alaska's first road, then known as the Valdez to Eagle Trail. Serving gold seekers and early settlers, the Roadhouse thrived throughout nine decades. In 1979, it was designated a national historic landmark. The original structure was destroyed by fire in 1992, but in 1994, the owners opened a small store on the site. About two years later, a new roadhouse began to take shape. Today, the Denton family carries on the longtime tradition of the Sourdough Roadhouse, including 107-year-old sourdough starter essential to their trademark pancakes. The new, improved roadhouse on the original, historic site is a must-stop for travelers at Milepost V 147.7 of the Richardson Highway.

McCarthy Road

Kennicott Glacier Lodge

The McCarthy Road connects Chitina, at the end of the Edgerton Highway, with a pedestrian bridge that crosses the Kennicott River and allows access to the town of McCarthy (a mile from the river) and historic Kennicott (5 miles away). This 59-mile gravel road follows the right-of-way of the Copper River & Northwestern Railway built in 1907 to carry copper ore from Kennicott to Cordova. Although the railway and mine ceased operation in 1938, railroad spikes still turn up regularly along the McCarthy Road, and the huge complex of barn-red buildings that make up Kennicott Mill is under restoration by the National Park Service.

BISCUITS

Rich and Jody Kirkwood
Kennicott Glacier Lodge
Kennicott, AK

1 cup **bread flour**
1 cup **pastry flour**
$1/4$ Tbs. (about 1 tsp.) **salt**
$1/2$ Tbs. (about 2 tsp.) **granulated sugar**
$1/2$ oz. (about 2 to 3 tsp.) **baking powder**
$1/4$ cup **shortening**
$1/4$ cup **butter, softened**
$3/4$ to 1 cup **buttermilk**

Combine all dry ingredients. Add butter and shortening to dry mixture and blend to a crumb mixture/texture. Add buttermilk and mix to form dough. On a floured surface, roll dough out to $1/2$" thick. Cut with biscuit cutter. Bake at 450°F for 10 to 12 minutes.

Yields 1 dozen biscuits.

CHOCOLATE KRINKLE COOKIES

Leslie Sorenson
Kennicott Glacier Lodge
Kennicott, AK

1/2 lb. butter
1 lb. granulated sugar
5 eggs
1 Tbs. vanilla
10 1/2 oz. cake flour
4 oz. cocoa
1/4 Tbs. salt
2/5 oz. baking powder
confectioner's sugar to garnish

Preheat oven to 350°F. Cream together butter and sugar, making sure there are no lumps. Add eggs and vanilla. Sift together dry ingredients and add to wet mixture. Do Not Overmix. Roll into balls. Roll in confectioner's sugar and place on baking sheet. Bake at 350°F.

Yields about 2 1/2 dozen.

CINNAMON BUNS

JoAnne Woolever
Kennicott Glacier Lodge
Kennicott, AK

Dough:
1 Tbs. **dry yeast**
1 cup **warm milk (105° to 110°F)**
1/2 cup **granulated sugar**
1/3 cup **melted margarine**
1 tsp. **salt**
2 **eggs**
4 cups **all-purpose flour**

Filling:
1/3 cup **soft margarine**
1 cup **nuts, chopped (optional)**
1 cup **brown sugar, packed**
1/4 cup **cinnamon**

For dough: Preheat oven to 350°F. Lightly grease or spray baking pan. In a large bowl, dissolve yeast in warm milk. Mix in sugar, margarine, salt and eggs. Add flour and mix well. Knead dough into a large ball. Cover the dough and let rise in a warm place about an hour or until dough has doubled in size. Roll dough out onto a lightly floured surface until it is approximately 21" long, 16" wide and 1/4" thick.

For filling: Spread 1/3 cup margarine evenly over surface of dough, then sprinkle on filling ingredients. Working carefully, roll dough from top (21" side) down to the bottom edge.

Cut rolled dough into 1 1/2" slices. (Dental floss or string works best; place it underneath the rolled dough, pull ends up and "tie.") Place buns, evenly spaced, in greased baking pans, allowing enough room for them to double in size. Allow buns to rise about 30 minutes or until doubled in size. Bake for 20 to 25 minutes (internal temperature of 180°F) or until lightly browned. Spread or drizzle your choice of topping *(one recipe follows)* while still slightly warm but not hot.

Yields 12 large rolls.

Topping:
1/2 cup **margarine, softened**
1 1/2 cups **confectioner's sugar**
1/4 cup **cream cheese**
1/2 tsp. **vanilla extract**
1/8 tsp. **salt**

In an electric mixer, beat ingredients together well until light and fluffy.

SNICKERDOODLE COOKIES

Leslie Sorensen
Kennicott Glacier Lodge
Kennicott, AK

1/2 cup **butter**
1/2 cup **shortening**
1 1/2 cups **granulated sugar**
2 **eggs**
2 3/4 cups **flour**
2/3 Tbs. **cream of tartar**
1/3 Tbs. **baking soda**
1/4 tsp. **salt**

For Dipping:
1/8 cup **granulated sugar**
1/8 cup **cinnamon**

Cream together butter, shortening and sugar (make sure there are no lumps). Add eggs. Sift together dry ingredients, add to wet mixture and mix well.

Mix together cinnamon and sugar for dipping. Roll dough into balls and roll in cinnamon-sugar mixture. Place on ungreased baking sheet about 2" apart. Bake at 400°F for 8 to 10 minutes until lightly browned but still soft. These cookies puff up at first, then flatten out with crinkled tops.

Yields about 5 dozen 2" cookies.

Denali Highway

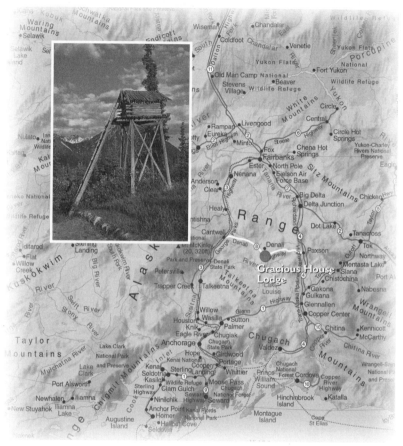

The 134-mile-long Denali Highway winds along the south flank of the Alaska Range, connecting the Richardson Highway at Paxson with the Parks Highway at Cantwell.

A mostly gravel road, closed by snow in winter, the Denali highway is a popular summer route for outdoor recreationists, offering spectacular mountain scenery, ORV and mountain biking trails, fishing, hunting and bird watching opportunities. The Denali Highway opened in 1957 as the first road link to Mount McKinley National Park (now Denali National Park and Preserve).

MONGOLIAN MOOSE

Carol Rhodes-Gratias
Gracious House Lodge
Mile P 82 Denali Highway

1 lb. moose steak
$1/4$ cup soy sauce
1 Tbs. dry sherry
1 Tbs. cornstarch
1 Tbs. brown sugar
2 tsp. crushed red pepper
4 to 6 whole red peppers
2 bunches green onions, slivered
2 yellow onions, sliced
3 cloves garlic, crushed
1 tsp. baking soda
1 tsp. sesame oil
$1/4$ cup plus 2 Tbs. peanut oil

Cut moose steak into very thin pieces and tenderize. Mix all ingredients except oil for marinade, and marinate meat for 30 minutes. Stir-fry in heated sesame and peanut oils until meat is done. Serve with rice.

Serves 4 to 6.

Steese Highway

The 162-mile Steese Highway links Fairbanks with Chena Hot Springs, Circle Hot Springs and Circle City on the Yukon River. The Steese follows the Chatanika River northeast of Fairbanks, crossing Cleary, Twelvemile and Eagle summits, 3 of Alaska's 10 highest highway passes.

The Steese Highway passes through an area rich in gold mining history: Chatanika Camp, Davidson Ditch, and the Discovery Claim, where Felix Pedro discovered gold in 1902, starting the gold rush that founded Fairbanks.

CANDY BAR SALAD

LaVerna Miller
Arctic Circle Hot Springs
Mile J 8.2 Circle Hot Springs Road

5 apples, diced (4 peeled, 1 with peel on for color)
1 small can crushed pineapple, well drained
1 cup regular salted shelled peanuts
4 Snickers® candy bars cut into bite-sized pieces
1 small carton Cool Whip® non-dairy whipped topping

Mix ingredients together and chill. Can be served as a salad or a dessert.

Serves 8 to 10.

Seward Highway

Girdwood Guest House
Alyeska Resort
The Bake Shop
Turnagain House
Summit Lake Lodge
Varly's Swiftwater Seafood Café
Bear's Den Bed & Breakfast

Gulf of Alaska

Recognized as one of the most scenic highways in the country, the 127-mile-long Seward Highway curves southeast from Anchorage along Turnagain Arm, before crossing an isthmus to the Kenai Peninsula and continuing south through the Kenai Mountains to Seward on Resurrection Bay. Roads branching off the Seward Highway provide access to Girdwood at the base of Mount Alyeska; to Portage Glacier and the port of Whittier; to historic Hope; and to Exit Glacier in Kenai Fjords National Park.

BERRY CRISP
Phillip Richter
Turnagain House
Mile S 103.1 Seward Highway

Filling:
1/2 tsp. lemon rind, grated
1/4 cup granulated sugar
1/4 cup brown sugar
1/4 cup flour
1/2 tsp. cinnamon
1/4 tsp. ground cloves
1 Tbs. instant tapioca
1 pint raspberries
1/2 pint blueberries
1/2 pint blackberries

Topping:
1/4 cup granulated sugar
1/4 cup brown sugar
1/2 tsp. cinnamon
1/2 tsp. salt
1/4 cup flour
1/4 cup rolled oats
1/8 cup butter, cold

For filling: Mix all filling ingredients except berries, then fold in berries until coated.

For topping: Combine sugars, spices, flour and oats. Cut in butter until mixture looks like meal.

Place filling in 6 6-oz. greased and sugar-coated ramekins. Top with topping and bake at 350°F for 20 minutes. Cool, and serve with ice cream.

Serves 6.

SOURDOUGH BREAD

Judy Jonsen
Girdwood Guest House
Girdwood, AK

"Girdwood Guest House, located in Girdwood, Alaska, serves guests authentic homemade sourdough bread each morning. This is made from sourdough starter kept active since the '70s. It is delicious and adapted for a bread maker that makes a 2-lb. loaf."

1 cup **sourdough starter** *(recipe on page 107)*
$3/4$ cup **warm water**
$1/4$ cup **warm water mixed with 1 tsp. baking soda**
3 $3/4$ cup **bread flour**
3 Tbs. **granulated sugar**
2 Tbs. **dry milk**
1 $1/2$ tsp. **salt**
2 Tbs. **butter**
2 tsp. **yeast**

Add all ingredients, except yeast, to your bread maker in the order listed. Make a well in the middle of the flour to add yeast. Do not let yeast touch any wet ingredients. In the bread maker, it takes 3 $1/2$ hours for mixing and baking.

Yields 1 loaf.

MEDALLIONS OF BUFFALO & ALASKA KING CRAB OSCAR

Rob Obermann, Executive Chef
Seven Glaciers Restaurant/Alyeska Resort
Girdwood, AK

Rob Obermann, executive chef at Alyeska Resort, says this recipe is a specialty at the scenic Seven Glaciers Restaurant.

White Truffle Béarnaise:
2/3 cup **dry white wine**
1 **shallot, minced**
2 Tbs. plus 2 tsp. **fresh tarragon, minced**
2 Tbs. plus 2 tsp. **fresh chervil, minced**
1/2 tsp. **white pepper**
2 **large egg yolks**
4 oz. **clarified butter**
8 oz. **truffle oil**
salt and cayenne pepper to taste

Buffalo medallions and crab:
8 2-oz. **buffalo medallions cut from buffalo tenderloin**
4 **large Alaska King crab legs**
1 dozen **asparagus spears, blanched**
2 Tbs. **olive oil**
fresh tarragon, salt and pepper to taste

For white truffle béarnaise: Simmer wine, shallot, herbs (2 Tbs. each tarragon and chervil) and white pepper until reduced to about 1/8 cup. Strain reduction through a fine sieve.

Place egg yolks into stainless steel bowl with a tablespoon of reduction.

Place bowl over a saucepan of barely simmering water, and beat the yolks with a whip until thickened and warm.

Temperature of yolks should be 145°F. Remove from heat, lift up bowl and place a clean, damp towel over the top and down under the saucepan. Set the bowl on top of the saucepan over the cloth, and pour the butter in a slow, steady stream while beating continuously. Add the truffle oil using the same procedure. As the mixture thickens, alternate the truffle oil with some of the reduction. Continue until all of the truffle oil and the reduction are emulsified. Add remaining herbs (2 tsp. each tarragon and chervil) and season to taste with salt and cayenne pepper. Adjust the thickness of the sauce by beating in additional warm water.

For buffalo medallions and crab: Heat oil in large non-stick skillet. Season each medallion, place in pan and cook until well browned on bottom. Turn meat over, and continue to cook to desired doneness. While medallions are cooking, cut crab legs in half. Boil or steam crab legs for approximately 6 to 8 minutes until heated through. Pull crabmeat out of half of the legs.

Place one buffalo medallion on center of hot plate. Place crabmeat and asparagus spears on medallion. Place second medallion on top of crabmeat and asparagus. Drizzle truffle béarnaise sauce over entire buffalo medallion. Garnish with other half of crab leg and fresh tarragon.

Serves 4.

CLAM CHOWDER

Michael Flynn
The Bake Shop
Girdwood, AK

$1/2$ lb. **butter**
4 **onions, diced small**
6 **potatoes, diced**
46 oz. **clam juice**
$1/4$ to $1/3$ cup **flour**
1 bag **celery, chopped**
51 oz. (1 large can) **clams, chopped in juice**
1 lb. **sour cream**
salt and white pepper to taste
lemon juice to garnish
parsley, chopped to garnish

Melt butter, add onions and cook on medium-low heat until tender and clear.

While onions sweat, put diced potatoes in pot. Cover with clam juice, and boil/simmer until tender. Set aside. Add flour to onion/butter mixture to form a roux. Add juice from chopped clams to form a thick base. Add cooked potatoes and celery. Bring temperature to 160° to 165°F and adjust consistency with clam juice or water. Add clams and sour cream. Season with salt and white pepper. Add a touch of lemon juice or chopped parsley to garnish if desired.

Yields 1 $1/2$ gallons.

RHUBARB CRISP

Don & Margaret Varlamos
Varly's Swiftwater Seafood Café
Whittier, AK

Crust:
3/4 lb. butter, melted
4 cups oatmeal
4 cups flour
4 cups brown sugar
1 Tbs. cinnamon
1/2 tsp. ground ginger
1/2 tsp. nutmeg
1/4 tsp. ground cloves

Syrup:
4 cups cold water
4 cups granulated sugar
2 tsp. vanilla
8 Tbs. cornstarch
16 cups rhubarb, cut into 1/2" pieces

Spray 12" X 24" pan with non-stick cooking spray. Mix crust ingredients until crumbly, and lightly press half of mixture into bottom of prepared pan. Mix the syrup ingredients together. Cook syrup until it just begins to thicken and remove from heat. Put rhubarb on crust in an even layer. Pour syrup over rhubarb and sprinkle remaining crust on top. Bake at 350°F for 3 hours.

(Recipe may be cut in half. Use an 8" X 13" pan and cook for 1 1/2 hours.)

Full recipe serves 32.

SUMMIT LAKE LODGE'S GRILLED STUFFED HALIBUT

June Arnoldy
Summit Lake Lodge
Mile S 45.8 Seward Highway

"A fresh, succulent halibut filet stuffed with bay shrimp, mushrooms, green onions and cheddar cheese, topped with our creamy mushroom sauce."

4 lbs. (64 oz.) halibut, 2 4-oz. pieces per serving

Stuffing:
1 1/2 Tbs. **butter**
1/3 cup **mushrooms, sliced**
1 clove **garlic, chopped**
1/4 tsp. **white pepper**
1 Tbs. **white wine**
1/4 Tbs. **clam base**
3 green onions, **chopped**
1 Tbs. **flour**
1/3 cup **half and half**
1/2 cup **bay shrimp**
2/3 cup **Panko bread crumbs**
1/3 cup **cheddar cheese, shredded**
mushroom cream sauce *(recipe follows)*

In a saucepan, combine butter, mushrooms, garlic, pepper, wine and clam base. Cook over low heat and reduce. Add onions, flour and half and half and stir until thickened.

Add shrimp and bread crumbs. Cool mixture in refrigerator and add cheese, reserving just enough to garnish.

Grill halibut. Put stuffing between 2 4-oz. pieces of halibut. Top with mushroom cream sauce and garnish with shredded cheddar cheese.

Mushroom Cream Sauce:
2 Tbs. flour
3 Tbs. butter
1 qt. milk
1/3 cup sliced mushrooms
1 Tbs. white wine
1 tsp. onion powder
1/2 bay leaf
1 Tbs. fresh garlic, chopped
1/4 tsp. salt
1/4 tsp. white pepper

In a double boiler over medium heat, cook flour and 2 tablespoons of butter together to make a roux. Gradually stir in warm milk. Cook over low heat for 1 hour, stirring frequently. In a separate pan, sauté mushrooms in wine and 1 tablespoon of butter. Add mushrooms to cream sauce and season.

Serves 8.

BANANA NUT BREAD

Shareen Adelmann
Bear's Den Bed & Breakfast
Seward, AK

1 cup **granulated sugar**
1/2 cup **butter**
2 **eggs**
2 cups **flour**
1/2 tsp. **baking soda**
1/2 tsp. **baking powder**
3 **ripe bananas, mashed**
1/2 cup **sour cream**
1 cup **walnuts, chopped**

Cream sugar, butter and eggs. Add flour, baking soda, baking powder and bananas and mix. Add sour cream and nuts and mix well.

Pour batter into greased loaf pan. Bake at 350°F for about 40 minutes or until a toothpick inserted in middle of loaf comes out clean.

Yields 1 loaf.

Sterling Highway

Mykel's Restaurant
Kenai Riverfront B&B
Alaska Inn Between B&B and Cabins
Longmere Lake Lodge B&B
Sunrise Inn
Kenai River Drifter's Lodge
Alaska Wildland Adventures
Clam Gulch Lodge   Gwin's Lodge & Restaurant
Skyline Bed and Breakfast
Spruce Acre Cabins
Land's End Resort
The Saltry
Tutka Bay Wilderness Lodge
Alaska Dancing Eagles B&B

of Alaska

From its junction with the Seward Highway at Tern Lake, the 143-mile Sterling Highway cuts west across the heart of the Kenai Peninsula to the Kenai/Soldotna area. From Soldotna, the Sterling Highway follows the west coast of the peninsula along Cook Inlet south to Homer.

Some of Alaska's most famous fishing spots are found along the Sterling Highway, including the Kenai and Russian rivers, Crooked Creek and Deep Creek. Roads branch off the main highway to campgrounds, hiking trails, rivers and lakes in Chugach National Forest and Kenai National Wildlife Refuge.

SPINACH-ARTICHOKE DIP

Mary Louise Molenda and Paula Shapro
Sunrise Inn
Mile S 44.9 Sterling Highway

7 9-oz. **sourdough bread rounds**
1 ¹/₂ oz. **butter**
¹/₂ **medium yellow onion,**
  chopped (medium dice)
¹/₂ **fresh jalapeño pepper,**
  finely chopped
1 tsp. **fresh garlic, chopped**
22 oz. **canned artichoke**
  hearts, drained

24 oz. **frozen spinach,**
  thawed and chopped
8 oz. **cream cheese**
2 ¹/₂ oz. **Parmesan cheese**
4 oz. **feta cheese**
¹/₂ cup **heavy cream**
splash of **Tabasco® sauce**
salt and pepper to taste

Cut the middle out of the sourdough round to make a bowl or
container to hold the dip. Slice the bread that came from the
middle of the bowl to use for dipping.

Melt butter in a heavy-bottomed saucepan over medium heat.
Add onion, jalapeño pepper and garlic. Cook until onions are
soft. Add artichoke hearts and spinach. Stir until smooth. Add
cheeses and cream, stirring until smooth and creamy. Add
Tabasco® sauce and salt and pepper to taste. Place bread bowl
in oven to warm. Heat dip in saucepan until warm and
creamy. Place bread bowl on a plate or platter or in a basket
and fill with 6 to 7 oz. of warm dip. Surround bread bowl
with sliced bread or fresh tortilla chips and serve warm.

Dip may be stored in a covered container in the refrigerator
for 4 to 5 days. Sourdough bread may be frozen and
thawed as needed for service.

HALIBUT TACOS

Melanie Bowman
Kenai River Drifter's Lodge
Mile S 48.3 Sterling Highway

2 lbs. halibut, skinned and cleaned
Cajun spice seasoning
3 Tbs. vegetable oil
1 large onion
jalapeños to taste
1 can Ortega® chilies, chopped
1 6-oz. can green enchilada sauce
1 dozen corn tortillas
lettuce
tomatoes
shredded cheese

Cover halibut on both sides with Cajun seasoning. Microwave until fish flakes, about 8 minutes. Set aside.

Sauté onions, jalapeños and chilies in oil, then add enchilada sauce. Cook on medium heat for 5 minutes. Add halibut and mix. Serve in warm tortillas with lettuce, tomatoes and cheese.

Serves 4.

FILET OF CARIBOU WITH WILD GAME SAUCE

Mitchell Cline
Alaska Wildland Adventures
Mile S 50.1 Sterling Highway

Caribou filet:
1 1/2 to 2 lbs. caribou tenderloin
  (beef or venison can be substituted)
2 to 3 cups of red wine
1 or 2 sprigs of fresh rosemary
1 or 2 sprigs of fresh thyme
3 or 4 cloves of garlic, minced
1 or 2 shallots, minced
1/2 tsp. dried mustard
1 tsp. sea salt
1 tsp. cracked black pepper
flour to season
salt and pepper to season
2 to 3 Tbs. olive oil

Wild game sauce:
4 to 8 oz. caribou trimmings, uncooked
2 to 3 oz. maple smoked bacon, uncooked
3 Tbs. vegetable oil
1 cup diced leeks
1 cup diced carrots
1 cup diced celery
4 oz. tomato paste
4 oz. port wine
2 cups water
1 cup heavy cream
1 or 2 cups wild mushrooms
2 or 3 Tbs. dried currants
salt and pepper to taste

Place the caribou in a small, deep pan. Then combine red wine, rosemary, thyme, garlic, shallots, dried mustard, sea salt and cracked pepper and pour over caribou. Marinate in refrigerator for at least 4 hours or overnight.

For wild game sauce: Combine and brown caribou trimmings and bacon in heavy stockpot with vegetable oil over medium-high heat. Add leeks, carrots and celery and cook for 2 to 3 minutes. Add tomato paste and cook for 1 to 2 minutes, stirring occasionally. (Allow sauce to thicken and begin to stick on the bottom, but do not burn.) Add port wine to deglaze. Cook for about 1 minute. Add water and bring to a boil, then lower heat and simmer (uncovered) for 30 minutes. Strain the sauce and reserve only the liquid. Combine the liquid and heavy cream, return to heat, bring to a boil and reduce to desired thickness. Sauté mushrooms and currants and add to sauce. Add additional port wine and salt and pepper to taste.

Slice caribou into 1/2"-thick medallions. Dust medallions with flour seasoned with salt and pepper. Add olive oil to a heated sauté pan and sear medallions on each side for 1 to 2 minutes over high heat until medium rare.

Arrange caribou medallions on a plate and cover with game sauce. For side dishes, serve wild rice or roasted potatoes with a vegetable medley of sautéed baby carrots, broccoli and yellow squash. Serve with a nice Cabernet or Zinfandel.

Serves 4 to 6.

ALASKAN STYLE CARROT CAKE

Shirley Siter
Gwin's Lodge & Restaurant
Mile S 52 Sterling Highway

"Many folks come to Gwin's just for this very special dessert that is the best carrot cake served in Alaska!"

Cake:
1 cup **salad oil**
2 cups **granulated sugar**
4 **eggs**
2 cups **flour**
2 tsp. **baking soda**
1 tsp. **salt**
2 tsp. **ground cinnamon**
1 tsp. **vanilla**
4 cups **carrots, shredded**
1 cup **walnuts, chopped**
8 oz. **crushed pineapple (drained)**

Icing:
1 lb. **solid butter or margarine**
3 lbs. **cream cheese**
2 tsp. **vanilla**
2 tsp. **lemon juice**
2 lbs. **confectioner's sugar**
1/2 cup **half and half**

For cake: Preheat oven to 350°F.

In a mixing bowl, beat oil and sugar until thick and opaque. Add eggs one at a time and beat until thoroughly mixed.

Slowly add dry ingredients followed by the vanilla. Add carrots, walnuts and pineapple while mixing to ensure uniform consistency.

Pour cake batter into greased bundt cake pan and bake at 355°F for 55 minutes. Remove from oven and allow to thoroughly cool before inverting onto large plate to frost. Frost only after cake is completely cool.

For icing: Beat butter or margarine and cream cheese together until soft. Add vanilla and lemon juice and slowly add confectioner's sugar until thoroughly mixed. Place icing in refrigerator until cool and firm before frosting the cake.

Serves 12 "Alaska-sized portions."

SMOKED ALASKAN SALMON CHOWDER

Robert Siter
Gwin's Lodge & Restaurant
Mile S 52 Sterling Highway

"Our No. 1 soup/chowder. A signature type menu item that many folks come a long distance for and ask, more than any other item, for our recipe."

10 strips **bacon**
2 **large onions, finely minced**
4 **celery stalks, finely minced**
3 **carrots, finely chopped**
5 **green onions, finely minced**
3/4 bunch **fresh parsley**
1/2 cup **water**
1/3 Tbs. **black pepper**
1 1/2 Tbs. **dry dill weed**
salt to taste
6 cups **fish broth (water mixed with fish base)**
8 **red potatoes, chopped**
1 cup **flour**
1 cup **butter**
5 cups **milk**
3/4 cup **white wine (optional)**
1/4 cup **lemon juice**
1 1/2 lbs. **Alaska smoked salmon**
   (sockeye salmon suggested), flaked
1 1/2 cups **corn kernels**

Chop (medium chop) bacon and sauté in a large pan with onions, celery, carrots, green onions and parsley. Sweat in a 1/2 cup of water and cover with lid.

Add spices and fish broth, then simmer until vegetables are tender. Add chopped red potatoes and simmer until they are also tender.

Mix flour and butter to form a roux. Mix roux with vegetables and simmer for 5 minutes. Remove vegetable mix and place in a medium-sized pot with milk. Over medium heat, stir constantly, bring mixture to temperature and allow to thicken slightly. Add white wine (if desired), lemon juice, flaked smoked salmon and corn. Continue to heat over medium heat, stirring constantly until chowder is to temperature. You may add a small amount of water to achieve desired thickness and consistency.

Serves 8.

CRAB SCRAMBLE

Pat Dwinnell
Longmere Lake Lodge B&B
Mile S 88 Sterling Highway

"This is a light and wonderful breakfast or brunch dish. Serve with fresh fruit, a muffin and freshly ground coffee."

9 eggs
$1/2$ cup **milk**
1 large package **cream cheese**
1 can **crab meat**
$1/4$ tsp. **salt**
$1/4$ tsp. **pepper**
$1/4$ lb. **butter**
1 Tbs. **fresh dill, chopped**

Beat together eggs, milk, cream cheese, crab, salt and pepper. Melt $1/4$ lb. butter in 12" x 7" pan. Pour mixture into pan and sprinkle dill on top. Bake at 350°F for $1/2$ hour.

Serves 8.

WILD RICE QUICHE

Pat Dwinnell
Longmere Lake Lodge B&B
Mile S 88 Sterling Highway

"A combination of wild rice, ham and spices makes this a hardy and tasty breakfast. Men do like this quiche."

1 unbaked pastry shell
1 cup wild rice, cooked
1/3 cup ham or bacon, chopped
1 small onion, finely chopped
1/4 cup light cream or milk
1/4 tsp. ground mustard
1/2 tsp. salt
dash of pepper
1 cup shredded Monterey Jack cheese
5 eggs
2 tsp. parsley
2 tsp. chives
1 tsp. tarragon

Bake the crust at 425°F for 5 minutes. Remove from oven. Reduce oven temperature to 350°F. Spoon the wild rice into the crust. In a skillet, sauté ham or bacon and onion until tender. Spoon into crust. Mix cream, mustard, salt and pepper and pour into crust.

Bake at 325°F for 35 minutes. Let stand for 5 minutes before cutting. Garnish with fresh fruit and serve with muffins or toast.

Serves 6.

MACADAMIA NUT CRUSTED HALIBUT

Chef Kevin Paulson
Mykel's Restaurant
Soldotna, AK

"This is one of our 2 favorite and most requested recipes at Mykel's."

4 6- to 7-oz. **halibut filets**
1 cup **macadamia nuts, crushed**
3/4 cup **Panko bread crumbs**
2 **eggs**
1 Tbs. **water**
seasoning salt
flour, for dredging
peanut oil, for sautéing
mango & papaya salsa *(recipe follows)*

Place macadamia nuts and Panko in food processor bowl fitted with a work blade, and using pulse, crush nuts and Panko together to achieve a medium coarseness. Do not over-grind nuts, or you will extract oil.

Beat eggs with water until smooth. Heat a large sauté pan or skillet on medium-low to medium heat. Lightly season halibut, dredge in flour, shake off excess and dip in egg mixture. Then, coat halibut well with nut mixture. Press mixture into filets, and lightly shake off excess. Add oil then halibut to the pan. Let filets brown 3 to 4 minutes, then turn them over. Continue cooking halibut until golden brown on both sides, approximately 6 to 8 minutes total time.

If using thick filets (1" or thicker), finish cooking in a 350°F oven for 7 to 10 minutes. Spoon mango & papaya salsa *(recipe follows)* over each filet.

Mango & Papaya Salsa—Hawaiian Style:
1 **papaya**
1 **mango**
3 Tbs. **sweet chili sauce**
1 can (11.5 oz.) **papaya nectar**
1 tsp. **mint flakes, crushed**
2 tsp. **pickled ginger, chopped**
$1/4$ tsp. **salt**

Peel and remove seeds from papaya and mango and cut into $1/2$" pieces. Place fruit in mixing bowl, add all other ingredients and mix well. Let set 2 hours. Can be made up to 5 days in advance. Serve at room temperature or just warm. Do not boil salsa; fruit will fall apart.

Serves 4.

WALNUT CRUSTED SALMON WITH RASPBERRY BEURRE BLANC

Chef Kevin Paulson
Mykel's Restaurant
Soldotna, AK

"This is one of our two favorite and most requested recipes at Mykel's."

Salmon:
1 6-oz. salmon filet, boneless and skinless
1/2 cup walnuts, chopped medium
1/8 cup bread crumbs
salt, pepper and granulated garlic (or seasoning salt blend) to season
flour to dredge
1 egg, beaten with splash of water
oil to cook salmon (Butter tends to burn; Chef Kevin uses peanut oil for this dish.)

Sauce:
1/2 cup white wine
1/4 cup heavy cream
1 1/4 cups raspberries
1/2 Tbs. honey
2 Tbs. unsalted butter, softened to room temperature

Preheat oven to 350°F.

Crush walnuts in food processor or with knife and mix with bread crumbs. Lightly season salmon with salt, pepper and garlic (or seasoning salt blend), dredge in flour and dunk in egg to coat.

Put salmon in walnut mix and gently press to cover filet.

Heat oil to medium heat on stovetop. Gently brown the filet, skin side up (approximately 3 minutes). Turn salmon over and brown on other side (3 minutes). Place filet on baking sheet and place in oven for 7 to 9 minutes or until done.

Pour wine into saucepan and reduce by one quarter. Add cream and raspberries and bring back to boil. Reduce again by one quarter. Add honey to taste. Reduce heat to medium, add butter and stir until incorporated into raspberry mixture. Remove salmon filet from oven and place it on a plate. Spoon sauce over top.

Serves 1.

CONSERVATION CORPS CHILI

Jim and Cindy Nelson
Kenai Riverfront B&B/RV Park
Mile SY 1.8 Kenai Spur Highway

"Grandpa Nelson handed down this recipe from his days in the 1930s and '40s working in the Conservation Corps in northern Minnesota as a camp cook. We've learned a lot about cooking for a crowd from Grandpa, and we enjoy it as much as he did!"

2 lbs. **ground beef**
2 **onions, finely chopped**
2 cloves **garlic, minced**
4 **celery stalks, chopped**
2 cans **tomatoes**
2 cans **kidney beans**
²/3 cup **ketchup**
2 tsp. **chili powder**
¹/2 tsp. **cayenne pepper**
¹/2 tsp. **black pepper**
water as needed

Brown beef with onion, garlic and celery. Add all remaining ingredients and cook slowly for a full day in a crock pot, Dutch oven or on the stove.

Serves 8 to 10.

GRANDPA'S ZESTY SPARERIBS

Jim and Cindy Nelson
Kenai Riverfront B&B/RV Park
Mile SY 1.8 Kenai Spur Highway

Ribs:
1 to 2 racks of spareribs, cut individually or in pairs
2 to 3 whole lemons, unpeeled, washed and thinly sliced
2 to 3 large sweet onions, thinly sliced

Sauce:
2 cups ketchup
2/3 cup Worcestershire sauce
1 1/2 tsp. chili powder
1 1/2 tsp. salt
2 heavy dashes Tabasco® hot sauce
2 cups water

For ribs: Place ribs in a shallow roasting pan or two, meaty side up. Cover with a layer of sliced lemons, then a layer of onions. Roast in a very hot oven (425°F) for 30 to 45 minutes, being careful not to burn the lemons or onions.

For sauce: Combine sauce ingredients in a saucepan and bring to a boil. Pour over the ribs in the roasting pans or transfer ribs to a crock pot or Dutch oven and cover with sauce. Continue baking at 350°F or in a slow-cooker. Baste ribs occasionally. Add more water if sauce gets too thick.

Serves 8 to 10.

FINNISH PASTIES

Jim and Cindy Nelson
Kenai Riverfront B&B/RV Park
Mile SY 1.8 Kenai Spur Highway

"This is by far our family's favorite dinner, going back to the turn of the century, when Great Grandpa Isacc Maki emigrated from Finland and started our family lineage in America. The miners and lumberjacks of Northern Minnesota would take pasties with them for a warm, hearty lunch, in a convenient stuffed pastry shell. We enjoy them today on fishing and hunting trips in Alaska, or just about anytime we can convince Mom to make them."

Pasty Crust:
1 1/2 cups **flour**
1/2 tsp. **salt**
1/3 cup **shortening or lard**
3 to 4 Tbs. **cold water**

Pasty Filling:
1 to 2 lbs. **tender moose, caribou or beef steak**
3 **medium potatoes, sliced small and thinly**
4 **carrots, sliced**
1 **onion, chopped**
1 **rutabaga, grated**
about 2 Tbs. **butter**
salt and pepper to taste

Cut shortening or lard into flour and salt to form pasty crust. Slowly add 3 to 4 Tbs. cold water to moisten. You can let the dough (moist but not sticky) sit out on the counter for a day or overnight to make it easier to roll out and flakier if you have the time.

Prepare filling ingredients by slicing vegetables, cutting meat into bite-sized pieces and grating the rutabaga.

Roll out pasty dough into a dinner-plate-sized circle and place it on a sheet of aluminum foil. Add a portion of filling ingredients to half of the surface of the crust. Add 2 slices of butter, season with salt and pepper and fold the other half of the crust over. Crimp the edge of the crust to form a seal. Slice top of crust like a pie for venting and fold up foil to cover. Bake at 350°F for 45 minutes. Open foil on top and bake an additional 10 to 15 minutes until golden brown. Pasties freeze and reheat well, so bake plenty!

Serves 8 to 10.

KENAI BLUEBERRY PIE

Jim and Cindy Nelson
Kenai Riverfront B&B/RV Park
Mile SY 1.8 Kenai Spur Highway

Pie crust:
1 1/2 cups **flour**
1/2 tsp. **salt**
2 tsp. **granulated sugar**
1/3 cup **shortening**
3 to 4 Tbs. **cold water**

Filling:
4 cups **blueberries**
1 1/2 cups **granulated sugar**
3 cups **flour**
1/2 tsp. **cinnamon**
1 to 2 Tbs. **butter**

For pie crust: Mix flour, salt, sugar, shortening and cold water together. Roll dough out and place in pie plate or pan.

For filling: Mix all filling ingredients and pour into unbaked pie crust. Dot filling with butter. Cover with top crust, cut vents and sprinkle with sugar. Bake at 425°F until browned. Cover lightly with foil if needed. Continue to bake until bubbly, about 35 to 45 minutes. Adjust temperature to 400°F if needed.

Serves 6 to 8.

NANATUZY'S SUPER CRISP SWEET PICKLES

Jim and Cindy Nelson
Kenai Riverfront B&B/RV Park
Mile SY 1.8 Kenai Spur Highway

"These pickles are known far and wide as some of the best sweet pickles ever tasted. They won first place in the Minnesota State Fair sometime in the '70s, and we use them today as a garnish, in homemade tartar sauce for our fish fries and as a base ingredient in other sauces and dressings. Seems like we run out each year, no matter how many jars Mom makes for us. This year, we hope to start making our own!"

4 quarts **small pickling cucumbers, thinly sliced**
2 **red peppers**
3 cloves **garlic, minced**
$1/3$ cup **canning salt**
5 cups **granulated sugar**
1 $1/2$ tsp. **turmeric**
1 $1/2$ tsp. **celery seeds**
2 Tbs. **mustard seeds**
3 cups **white vinegar**

Combine cucumbers, red peppers and garlic. Cover with ice and canning salt. Let stand for 5 hours or overnight. Drain thoroughly. Combine and add remaining ingredients. Heat to a boil. Seal in hot, sterilized jars, cover and turn upside-down for 5 minutes.

Yields 8 pints. (But, according to Jim, you'll need more to get through a long Alaska winter.)

FISH FRY FRYDAYS

Jim and Cindy Nelson
Kenai Riverfront B&B/RV Park
Mile SY 1.8 Kenai Spur Highway

"This recipe is our own creation, based on cooking techniques for fish and meat that we learned while living in Tokyo, Japan, combined with our long heritage of Minnesota Walleye Fish Fry Fridays. You can be sure to find a variation of this served almost every Friday year-round at Kenai Riverfront. While we typically use halibut, it also works well with salmon, shrimp and clams or just about any hearty fish. Many first-time halibut eaters say this is the best fish they've ever had."

Fish:
2 lbs. boneless, skinless fresh Alaska fish filets
1 cup seasoned flour (flour, seasoning salt, lemon pepper, etc.)
2 eggs
splash of lemon and/or malt vinegar
touch of honey
2 cups Panko bread crumbs
2 quarts cooking oil (vegetable, peanut or olive)

Homemade tartar sauce:
1 cup Miracle Whip® sandwich spread
1/3 cup sweet pickles or relish
1 Tbs. lemon juice and/or 1 Tbs. malt vinegar
1 Tbs. dill, chopped (optional)

For fish: Use 3 good-sized plastic or glass containers to bread the fish for frying (Jim uses 3 rectangular plastic Ziploc® containers). Put the seasoned flour (flour, seasoning salt, lemon pepper and any other seasonings you like, e.g. Cajun seasoning, dill weed, etc.) in one container. In second container, beat eggs with lemon juice and/or malt vinegar and honey. Put bread crumbs in third container.

Coat each piece of fish with flour, then egg, then bread crumbs. Coat all fish and begin frying in oil at about 335°F. Fish should turn brown quickly but not burn. Turn fish over once, so both sides are golden brown.

For tartar sauce: Mix all tartar sauce ingredients well in a food processor.

Serve fish with tartar sauce and home fries for a great Fryday Fishfry!

Serves about 6 to 8.

"*I use some leftover tartar sauce mixed with some extra pickles and leftover grilled fresh king salmon to make a great salmon spread for crackers or sandwiches. It is very good, even better than I thought it would be. This recipe works, and my kids even like it!*"

SWEET CORN BREAD

Jim and Cindy Nelson
Kenai Riverfront B&B/RV Park
Mile SY 1.8 Kenai Spur Highway

1 cup **cornmeal**
3 cups **flour**
1 1/3 cups **granulated sugar**
2 Tbs. **baking powder**
1 tsp. **salt**
2/3 cup **olive oil**
4 **eggs**
2 1/2 cups **milk**
6 Tbs. **butter, melted**

Lightly grease a 9" X 13" baking pan. Mix all dry ingredients in a large bowl. Mix all wet ingredients in a small bowl, adding melted butter last. Combine all ingredients together and mix until well-combined. Bake at 350°F for 35 minutes. Serve with honey and butter.

Serves 8 to 10.

WILD BLUEBERRY PANCAKES

Jim and Cindy Nelson
Kenai Riverfront B&B/RV Park
Mile SY 1.8 Kenai Spur Highway

"Grandpa Nelson handed this recipe down from the days when he used to have a big pancake feed for all the family on Saturday mornings. We serve them now in our B&B and have our own pancake feeds now and then. We pick fresh wild blueberries every year on the Kenai Peninsula from the end of July through September."

1 **egg, beaten**
2 Tbs. **brown sugar**
1 cup **milk**
1 tsp. **vanilla**
1 cup **self-rising flour**
1/2 cup **blueberries**

Beat egg and brown sugar together. Add milk and vanilla. Slowly add flour to make a lumpy batter. Pour by ladle-full onto greased hot griddle. Sprinkle with blueberries. Flip once when brown and serve with blueberry syrup.

Serves 4.

FRESH APPLE CAKE

Barbara Schuerger
Alaska Inn Between B&B and Cabins
Mile S 18.7 Kalifornsky Beach Road

4 cups **diced apples**
2 cups **granulated sugar**
¹/2 cup **oil**
2 cups **nuts (pecans, filberts or Brazil nuts)**
2 **eggs, beaten**
2 cups **flour**
2 tsp. **baking soda**
2 tsp. **cinnamon**
¹/2 tsp. **salt**

Mix together apples, sugar, oil, nuts and eggs. Sift together flour, baking soda, cinnamon and salt and add to apple mixture. Batter will be thick. Pour batter into well-greased and floured cake pan. Bake at 350°F for 45 minutes or until a toothpick inserted into the middle comes out clean. This cake is good with buttercream frosting.

Serves 6 to 8.

HALIBUT ARTICHOKE DIP

Kelly Warwick
Clam Gulch Lodge
Mile S 119.6 Sterling Highway

"This is also good as a sandwich spread after the party."

1 to 2 lbs. **cooked halibut**
1 cup **Monterey Jack cheese, shredded**
8 oz. **cream cheese**
2 cups **mayonnaise**
1/2 cup **Parmesan cheese**
1 large can **artichoke hearts packed in water**
1 to 2 **jalapeño peppers, finely chopped**
2 cloves **garlic, crushed**
1 tsp. **Cajun seasoning**

Add all ingredients to saucepan. Cook on low heat until cheeses are melted. Stir often. Serve warm with sliced baguette bread or crackers.

Serves 10.

MORNING PIZZA

Karen Cauble
Skyline Bed and Breakfast
Homer, AK

1 tube **refrigerated crescent rolls**
3 **eggs, beaten**
1/4 cup **milk**
salt and pepper to taste
1 cup **frozen hash brown potatoes, thawed**
1 small can **sliced mushrooms, drained**
3 **green onions, chopped**
1 cup **medium or sharp cheddar cheese, shredded**

Separate crescent roll dough into 8 triangles. Place in an ungreased pizza pan with points toward center. Press over bottom of pan, joining together dough to form crust with scalloped edge. Mix eggs, milk and salt and pepper and pour into crust. Sprinkle with potatoes, mushrooms and green onions. Top with cheddar cheese. Bake at 375°F for 30 minutes.

Serves 6 to 8.

Banana Nut Bread

Joyce Williams
Spruce Acre Cabins
Homer, AK

"This is the recipe I use the most. Everyone loves it."

1/2 cup **shortening**
1 cup **granulated sugar**
2 **eggs**
2 to 3 **crushed bananas**
1 small jar **cherries and juice**
2 cups **flour**
1 tsp. **baking soda**
1 tsp. **salt**
1 cup **nuts, chopped**

Cream shortening and sugar. Add eggs and beat well. Add bananas, cherries and cherry juice. Add dry ingredients and mix well. Add nuts and pour into well-greased bread pans. (I use 4 small bread pans for my cabins.) Bake at 350°F for 30 minutes. Remove from pans and let cool on wire rack.

Yields 4 small loaves or 1 large loaf.

MOCHA

Joyce Williams
Spruce Acre Cabins
Homer, AK

"I have this mocha in each one of my cabins, and everyone loves it and wants the recipe."

2 cups **Carnation® hot chocolate mix**
1 cup **Coffeemate® creamer**
1 cup **granulated sugar**
1 cup **instant coffee**
1 cup **hot water**

Mix all dry ingredients together well. Put 2 to 4 tablespoons in a coffee cup. Add hot water to fill the cup and stir until mix is dissolved.

Serves about 20.

HOT CRAB AND ARTICHOKE DIP

Dawn Schneider
Land's End Resort
Homer, AK

"This dip has other uses too! Stuff a salmon filet, top a halibut filet, or use as a sandwich spread with lettuce and tomato. Enjoy!"

1 cup **sour cream**
$1/2$ cup **mayonnaise**
4 oz. **cream cheese**
2 10-oz. jars **artichoke hearts**
1 **onion, minced**
$1/2$ cup **Parmesan cheese**
salt and white pepper to taste
1 Tbs. **Tabasco® hot sauce**
2 lbs. **crab meat**
seasoned bread crumbs
$1/8$ cup **fresh parsley, chopped**

Whip sour cream, mayonnaise and cream cheese together until well blended. Chop artichoke hearts, drain well and add to whipped mixture. Add onions and Parmesan cheese, reserving 3 Tbs. of cheese to sprinkle on top. Add salt and pepper and hot sauce and mix well. Add crabmeat and mix 1 minute. Pour dip into buttered casserole dish and cover with bread crumbs and reserved Parmesan cheese. Bake at 350°F for 15 minutes, until top is golden brown. Garnish with chopped parsley.

Serves 4 to 6.

CIOPPINO

Marian Beck, from
Salmon Patties and Rosehip Pie, **The Saltry**
Halibut Cove, AK

¹/₈ cup **oil**
2 Tbs. **butter**
1 **large white onion, peeled and finely chopped**
2 cloves **garlic, minced**
1 **medium carrot, finely chopped**
¹/₂ **medium green pepper, chopped**
¹/₂ **medium red pepper, chopped**
1 **small leek, finely chopped (white part only)**
1 **small celery stalk, chopped**
2 28-oz. cans **diced tomatoes, including liquid**
8 oz. **dry white wine**
¹/₈ cup **honey**
1 Tbs. **basil (¹/₄ cup if fresh)**
1 Tbs. **oregano (¹/₄ cup if fresh)**
1 tsp. **thyme (1 Tbs. if fresh)**
4 bay **leaves**
dash cayenne pepper
salt and black pepper to taste
1 lb. **clams**
1 lb. **mussels, de-bearded and cleaned**
1 lb. **halibut, cut into bite-sized pieces**

In a large pot, heat oil and butter and add onion, garlic, carrot, peppers, leek and celery. Sauté until soft. Add tomatoes, wine, honey and spices. Simmer 1 hour. Add clams, mussels and halibut and simmer an additional 10 to 15 minutes or until fish flakes when prodded with a fork and mussels and clams open. Be careful not to overcook.

Serves 8 to 10.

SMOKING FISH

Marian Beck, from
Salmon Patties and Rosehip Pie, **The Saltry**
Halibut Cove, AK

"Smoking fish makes a wonderful accent to any dish, or is a terrific appetizer or snack on its own. There are a number of home smokers available; the price varies widely as does the capacity. Standards used up here are the Little Chief and Big Chief electric smokehouses, or you can make your own. Experiment with the type of chips you use from the wide variety available. At the Saltry, we usually use cherry or alder chips.

"It is possible to smoke any type of fish, though not all of them hold smoked flavor well. At the Saltry, we regularly use smoked salmon and smoked black cod and have tried (and enjoyed) smoked shark. Below is a standard marinade that always works well and always tastes good."

Candied Salmon:
4 lbs. salmon or other fish, cut into 1"-wide boneless strips
1 cup soy sauce
1/2 onion
1 Tbs. garlic, minced
1 2" cube fresh ginger, skinned
1 cup brown sugar

Combine soy sauce, onion, garlic and ginger in a blender. Form a paste by mixing the liquid with the brown sugar. Slather fish with the paste and refrigerate for 3 days or until fish strips are stiff. Smoke fish according to smokehouse directions.

PICKLED SALMON

Marian Beck, from
Salmon Patties and Rosehip Pie, **The Saltry**
Halibut Cove, AK

"Pickled salmon in a glass jar makes a beautiful gift."

6 cups **salted fish, cut into 1" cubes**
1 gallon **white vinegar**
5 cups **granulated sugar**
1 cup **pickling spices**
8 cups **onion, sliced**

Cover salted fish with $1/2$ gallon vinegar and let sit for 24 hours.

Dump vinegar off fish and dispose of it. Boil remaining $1/2$ gallon of vinegar with sugar and spices to make brine. In a prepared pickling bucket or covered container, stack fish in alternating layers with liberal amounts of onion. Pour brine over fish and keep refrigerated for 2 weeks.

SALTRY BREAD

Marian Beck, from
Salmon Patties and Rosehip Pie, **The Saltry**
Halibut Cove, AK

"This is a Saltry original with a sweet and nutty flavor."

4 cups **warm water**
1/8 cup **yeast**
1 cup **honey**
1 cup **molasses**
6 cups **whole wheat flour**
1/3 cup **equal parts millet, sesame seeds and wheat bran**
6 cups **white flour**
2 Tbs. **salt**

Preheat oven to 350°F.

Start with all ingredients at room temperature. Dissolve yeast into water and add honey, molasses, salt and wheat flour. Mix in millet, sesame seeds and wheat bran. Let rise until doubled in size, then mix in white flour, adding one cup at a time. Let dough double in size again, then knead heavily for at least 5 minutes. Shape into loaves. Bake for 20 minutes, then lower temperature to 250°F and bake until brown.

Yields 4 to 6 loaves.

SALMON PATE

Marian Beck, from
Salmon Patties and Rosehip Pie, **The Saltry**
Halibut Cove, AK

"This pate makes a wonderful dish for a party. Serve with crackers or thinly sliced, toasted bread rounds. Garnish with chopped scallions or parsley and edible flowers, such as nasturtiums."

1 **medium red onion, halved**
1 **lb. smoked salmon** *(see recipe for Smoking Fish on page 191)*
3 **lbs. cream cheese, softened at room temperature**
1 **cup sour cream**
1 **Tbs. paprika**
1 **tsp. lemon juice**
1 **Tbs. tomato paste or juice**
3 **scallions, chopped**

Place half of the red onion in a food processor with 1 cup of smoked salmon. Puree and set aside.

Beat cream cheese for 5 minutes. Add sour cream, paprika, lemon juice, tomato paste or juice and pureed onion and salmon mix and beat for 1 more minute. Dice remaining onion and salmon into small pieces. By hand, stir the scallions, diced onion and diced salmon into the puree mixture. The pate should be stiff, not runny, when finished.

Serves 20.

SALTRY SUMMER SOUP

Marian Beck, from
Salmon Patties and Rosehip Pie, **The Saltry**
Halibut Cove, AK

3 cups **water**
3 cups **chicken stock**
1 **small ginger root, sliced**
3/4 cup **fresh or frozen peas**
3/4 cup **carrots, slivered**
1/2 cup **red pepper, slivered**
1 cup **corn**
1/2 cup **scallions, chopped**
cilantro, chopped to garnish
peanuts, chopped to garnish

In a soup pot, bring water and chicken stock to a boil. Add all ingredients except cilantro and peanuts. Simmer for 10 minutes. Garnish with cilantro and peanuts and serve.

Serves 8 to 10.

TONI'S COVE STYLE APPLE PIE

Marian Beck, from
Salmon Patties and Rosehip Pie, **The Saltry**
Halibut Cove, AK

Filling:
6 cups **tart apples (about 5 Granny Smith apples),
   peeled, cored and sliced**
1 cup **brown sugar**
1 Tbs. **cinnamon**
1 Tbs. **lemon juice**
1 tsp. **lemon zest**
1/4 tsp. **vanilla**

Grandma's Pie Crust:
1 cup **flour**
1 Tbs. **cornstarch**
1/2 tsp. **salt**
7 Tbs. **vegetable shortening**
1/4 cup **cold milk**

Preheat oven to 425°F.

For filling: Mix all filling ingredients together in medium-sized bowl and let sit while preparing crust.

For Grandma's Pie Crust: Whisk together flour, cornstarch and salt. Add shortening and mix with a fork until shortening is coated with flour mixture and forms small flaky pieces. Add milk a little at a time while continuing to mix gently. Pick up dough carefully with floured hands and form into a ball. Divide in half. Roll each ball out on a floured surface.

Lightly grease a pie pan with shortening. Line with bottom crust. Fill with apple filling and drizzle any remaining juice over apples. Cover with top crust, crimp edges and prick the top with a fork. Bake for 20 minutes, reduce heat to 350°F and bake another 30 to 35 minutes until crust is golden brown. Let cool and serve with vanilla ice cream or a slice of cheddar cheese.

Serves 8.

CHOCOLATE LILY CAKE
Jon & Nelda Osgood
Tutka Bay Wilderness Lodge
Kachemak Bay, AK

"Named after a brown lily that grows wild in Alaska, this rich and moist cake is simple to make from scratch."

Cake:
2 cups **all-purpose flour**
1 cup **granulated sugar**
1/3 cup **baking cocoa powder, unsweetened**
1 Tbs. **dry instant coffee**
2 tsp. **baking soda, sifted**
1/4 tsp. **salt**
1 cup **mayonnaise**
1 cup **water**
1 tsp. **vanilla**

Frosting:
6 Tbs. **butter or margarine, softened**
3/4 cup **baking cocoa powder, unsweetened**
1 Tbs. **dry instant coffee**
2 2/3 cups **confectioner's sugar, unsifted**
1/3 cup **milk**
1 tsp. **vanilla**

For cake: In a medium-sized bowl, combine all dry cake ingredients. Stir in mayonnaise, water and vanilla. Mix well. Pour batter into lightly oiled 9" X 13" baking pan. Bake at 350°F for 40 minutes or until a toothpick inserted in the middle comes out clean.

For frosting: In a small bowl, whip butter. Gradually add cocoa, coffee and confectioner's sugar alternately with milk. Beat mixture to a spreading consistency. Add a little more milk if needed. Blend in vanilla.

Let cake cool before frosting.

Serves 12.

CORN POLENTA PUDDING

Jon & Nelda Osgood
Tutka Bay Wilderness Lodge
Kachemak Bay, AK

"This is a hearty side dish especially good with salmon."

1/4 cup **butter or vegetable oil**
1/2 cup **onion, chopped**
1/4 cup **green pepper, chopped**
2 Tbs. **pimiento, chopped**
2 **eggs**
2 cans (14 oz.) **cream-style corn**
1/3 cup **dry corn meal**
1/4 tsp. **white pepper**

Sauté onion, green pepper and pimiento in butter.

In a medium-sized bowl, beat eggs. Add corn, corn meal, pepper and sautéed vegetables. Combine all ingredients well and pour into oil-sprayed 8" X 8" baking dish. Bake at 350°F for 1 hour or until firm.

Serves 6 to 8.

HALIBUT CEVICHE

Jon & Nelda Osgood
Tutka Bay Wilderness Lodge
Kachemak Bay, AK

Fish marinade:
1/2 lb. **skinless halibut, previously frozen**
1/4 cup **bottled lemon juice**
1/4 cup **bottled lime juice**

Vegetable mixture:
1/2 cup **green pepper, chopped**
1/2 cup **mushrooms, sliced**
1 **tomato, diced**
1/4 cup **ketchup**
1/2 tsp. **hot sauce**
1/2 tsp. **salt**
1/8 tsp. **dried oregano**
2 tsp. **Worcestershire sauce**
1/2 cup **black olives, sliced**

1 **can (14.5 oz.) stewed tomatoes, pureed in blender**
1/2 cup **onion, chopped**
3 Tbs. **olive oil**
6 **pimiento-stuffed green olives, sliced**
1/8 tsp. **dried basil**
1 Tbs. **fresh cilantro, chopped (may substitute parsley)**

Cut halibut into 1/4" cubes and put into glass bowl. Mix lemon and lime juices and stir into halibut. The juices should completely cover the fish. Marinate 3 hours in refrigerator, stirring occasionally.

In another bowl, gently mix all vegetable mixture ingredients together and refrigerate for 3 hours.

After 3 hours, drain fish and fold carefully into vegetable mixture. Serve chilled with tortilla chips. Ceviche can be refrigerated for 36 hours.

Serves 6.

LEMON PASTA

Jon & Nelda Osgood
Tutka Bay Wilderness Lodge
Kachemak Bay, AK

"Lemon, garlic and Romano cheese–so good with seafood."

1 lb. **capellini pasta**
zest and juice of 1 lemon
4 Tbs. **unsalted butter or olive oil**
1/4 tsp. **garlic salt**
1 tsp. **minced fresh garlic**
1/4 cup **Romano cheese, finely grated**
2 Tbs. **fresh parsley, chopped**

Cook pasta al dente. Drain, toss with a little olive oil and keep warm. In a small bowl, mix lemon juice and zest. In a frying pan, heat butter or olive oil over medium-low heat. Add cooked pasta, tossing constantly until warmed through. Add lemon juice mixture and toss. Sprinkle with garlic salt, fresh garlic, Romano and parsley. Toss and serve.

Serves 6.

POACHED KACHEMAK BAY SALMON

Jon & Nelda Osgood
Tutka Bay Wilderness Lodge
Kachemak Bay, AK

1 4- to 6-lb. **salmon, whole and dressed**
sufficient water to cover fish
4 Tbs. **pickling spices**

1 Tbs. **salt**
2 Tbs. **vinegar**

Fit fish into an oblong poacher or roasting pan large enough to hold it without crowding. The head may need to be removed. Leave the tail on, if possible, or partially sever the tail, and fold it back (it can be unfolded after cooking). Take fish out of pan and set aside.

Fill poaching pan with 1" of water. Add pickling spices, salt and vinegar and simmer for 10 minutes. Place fish in the pan and add just enough water to cover. Cover pan and simmer 20 minutes. Remove from heat and let stand 20 minutes. Test for doneness with a thermometer (fish should be 140° to 145°F in the thickest part). Return to heat if necessary and simmer until desired temperature is reached. Remove fish from liquid, drain and skin.

Serve hot or chilled, garnished with lemon slices and fresh dill or parsley. Serve with curried mayonnaise (stir 1/4 tsp. curry powder into 1 cup mayonnaise).

Serves 6 to 8.

TUTKA BAY
BAKED OATMEAL

Jon & Nelda Osgood
Tutka Bay Wilderness Lodge
Kachemak Bay, AK

3 cups **dry oatmeal**
1/3 cup **brown sugar**
2 tsp. **baking powder, sifted**
1 tsp. **salt**
1/4 tsp. **nutmeg**
1/2 tsp. **cinnamon**
2 **eggs, beaten (or 4 egg whites, beaten)**
1/2 cup **canola oil**
1 cup **milk (or water)**
1/2 tsp. **vanilla**
1/2 cup **walnuts, coarsely chopped**

In a medium-sized bowl, mix together oatmeal, brown sugar, baking powder, salt, nutmeg and cinnamon. In another medium-sized bowl, beat together eggs, oil, milk and vanilla. Stir liquid mixture into oatmeal mixture and mix well. Pour batter into oiled 2-quart baking dish. Sprinkle with chopped nuts. Bake at 350°F for 30 minutes. Spoon into cereal bowls and serve with milk.

Add raisins, chopped apple, diced banana, chopped dates or shredded coconut as desired.

Serves 9.

DANCING EAGLES SCONES

Judith W. Lethin
Alaska Dancing Eagles B&B
& Cabin Rentals
Seldovia, AK

"We get raves on these scones, especially from our British and European guests! They say they're the best they've ever had!"

2 1/4 cups **Bisquick® biscuit mix**
1/2 cup **granulated sugar**
1/4 cup **soft butter**
1/4 cup **sour cream**
1/2 cup **blueberries**
1 tsp. **vanilla**
1/2 cup (scant) **water**

Mix Bisquick®, sugar, butter, sour cream and blueberries together. Add vanilla and scant 1/2 cup water. Knead dough 6 to 8 times until biscuit consistency. Pat into a circle 8 to 10" in diameter. Cut into 8 wedges. Place onto parchment-covered baking sheet. Bake at 375°F for 15 to 18 minutes. Dust with confectioner's sugar.

Serves 8.

Prince William Sound

Southcentral Alaska's Prince William Sound is a 70-mile-wide gulf bounded to the north by the snow-capped Chugach Mountains and separated from the Gulf of Alaska to the south by Montague and Hinchinbrook islands. State ferries provide cross-sound transportation between the communities of Whittier, Valdez and Cordova. Major attractions in Prince William Sound are its wildlife and glaciers. Sightseeing cruises take in sea birds, sea otters, sea lions, whales and the Sound's star attraction, Columbia Glacier, one of Alaska's largest tidewater glaciers.

LAKEHOUSE MOOSE STEW VIA CROCK POT

John Devens
The Lakehouse
Valdez, AK

2 to 4 Tbs. **oil**
2 lbs. **lean moose (beef may be substituted), cut into 1" cubes**
1/4 cup **flour**
3 cans **beef broth**
1 can **tomato sauce**
2 medium **onions, quartered**
4 medium **carrots, cut into 1/2" pieces**
1 cup **celery, cut into 1/2" pieces**
6 medium **red or white potatoes, cubed**
1/4 cup **granulated sugar**
1/2 cup **frozen corn**
1/2 cup **frozen peas**
3 Tbs. **chives, fresh or dried**
salt and pepper to taste

Brown meat in a frying pan in oil. Meat should be brown on all sides. Mix flour, beef broth and tomato sauce until smooth and place in crock pot. Add browned moose (or beef) and all other ingredients. Mix well and cook on low heat for 6 to 8 hours.

Serves 6.

Inside Passage

Alaska's Inside Passage, located in the southeastern section of the state, is a unique region made up of thousands of islands and a mainland hemmed in by steep coastal mountains.

Because this spectacular topography prohibits road building between many communities, most Southeast towns are served by the state's ferry system, which connects mainline ports along the Inside Passage. This sheltered water route and the natural beauty of the Inside Passage also bring thousands of cruise ship passengers to Southeast every summer. Large and small cruise ships offer sightseeing trips to major Southeast attractions not served by the state ferry, including Glacier Bay National Park and Misty Fjords National Monument.

GRILLED ALASKA SALMON WITH SAUTÉED ORANGES

Carole Denkinger
Alaska Ocean View Bed & Breakfast Inn
Sitka, AK

4 salmon steaks or 1 lb. salmon filet, quartered
3/4 cup fresh-squeezed orange juice
2 Tbs. fresh chopped cilantro
2 cloves garlic, minced
1 tsp. sesame seeds
1/2 tsp. vegetable oil
1/4 tsp. ground cumin
1/4 tsp. crushed red pepper
3 oranges, peeled and thinly sliced

Arrange salmon steaks in a non-metal dish. In a small bowl, stir together orange juice, cilantro, garlic, sesame seeds, vegetable oil, cumin and pepper until well blended. Pour mixture over salmon, cover and refrigerate 30 minutes to 2 hours.

Preheat broiler or barbecue (we recommend using a grill basket if barbecuing). Drain marinade from salmon, reserving it. Broil salmon, without turning, about 10 minutes until fish flakes easily, brushing twice with reserved marinade. As salmon cooks, pour 1/3 cup of the marinade mixture into a skillet and add orange slices. Cook and toss gently over medium heat about 5 minutes. Serve salmon with orange slices and sauce.

Serves 4.

SAUTÉED FIDDLEHEADS

Davita Marchbanks
Glacier Bay Country Inn
Gustavus, AK

"Fiddleheads are the young shoots of wild ferns. They are prevalent in the area around the Glacier Bay Country Inn in early to mid-spring. They are delicious chilled in a salad or sautéed as a side dish. They should be picked 3 to 8 inches from the top and cleaned well (remove any dirt or brown fuzz). Blanching eases cleaning."

"Here's some fun with fiddleheads"

2 Tbs. butter, clarified
32 fiddleheads, blanched
1 clove garlic, chopped
salt and pepper to taste

In a large skillet, heat butter over medium-high heat. Add fiddleheads and sauté to coat with butter and garlic. Cook until fiddleheads are heated through. Season with salt and pepper and serve immediately.

Serves 4.

GLACIER BAY COUNTRY INN GRANOLA

Davita Marchbanks
Glacier Bay Country Inn
Gustavus, AK

"This is a big hit with our breakfast crowds! The sesame seeds and the Grand Marnier® add a special something to this unique version of granola, made unique by our former breakfast chef, Laurie Ross.

"Lumps? Here's Laurie's advice: 'It's just like the difference between baking a hard cookie or a soft cookie. The longer you bake it, the crispier and less lumpy it will get—but don't forget to stir!'

"This is also the official granola recipe of South Pole Station, Antarctica—thank you very much!"

3 cups **rolled oats**
$^1/_4$ cup **raw almonds, sliced**
$^1/_2$ cup **raw cashews, chopped**
$^1/_4$ cup **sesame seeds**
$^1/_4$ cup **raw sunflower seeds**
$^1/_2$ cup **dried coconut**
$^1/_4$ cup **dried date pieces**
$^1/_4$ cup **raisins and/or dried cranberries**
$^1/_4$ cup **light oil**
$^1/_4$ cup **brown sugar**
$^1/_4$ cup **honey**
$^1/_4$ cup **maple syrup**
2 Tbs. **molasses**
1 $^1/_2$ tsp. **vanilla extract**
1 tsp. **cinnamon**
$^1/_2$ tsp. **salt**
dash **of Grand Marnier®**

Preheat oven to 350°F.

In separate pans, oven roast oats, almonds, cashews, sesame seeds and sunflower seeds until lightly toasted. (Remove each pan as it's finished.) Set aside until cool. In a large bowl, combine all toasted ingredients with the coconut and set aside.

Combine oil, brown sugar, honey, molasses, vanilla, cinnamon and salt in a saucepan. Stir over low heat until well combined and warm to the touch (Do not boil!). Add Grand Marnier® and stir. Pour liquid mixture over dry mixture, and mix well. Turn out and flatten onto greased sheet pan, and roast at 350°F for about 30 minutes, stirring every 5 minutes (longer for crunchy granola, shorter for softer granola). Remove from oven and mix in raisins and dates. Cool and store in tightly sealed containers in a cool, dry place.

Yields about 1/2 gallon.

MARINATED TRI-TIP LONDON BROIL

Davita Marchbanks
Glacier Bay Country Inn
Gustavus, AK

"One of our most popular meat offerings (especially with the staff!), this works out great for a dinner entrée or leftover for awesome sandwiches. An insta-ready thermometer will help you make this roast come out perfect every time."

1 **whole tri-tip (coulotte) roast, trimmed of most of the excess fat**

Marinade:
1 bottle **Alaskan**® **Amber Ale (or other amber ale)**
1 ¹/2 cups **Teriyaki base** *(recipe follows)*
2 Tbs. **whole grain mustard**

Combine all marinade ingredients. Marinate roast overnight, turning once.

Preheat barbecue grill to high and oven to 400°F. Grill roast until nicely browned on outside. Remove to roasting pan with a rack, and place in oven until done to an internal temperature of 130°F (medium-rare), about 35 minutes. Allow to rest out of oven for 10 minutes before slicing into thin slices, cutting against grain of meat. Be sure to reserve all meat juices for a nice ale au jus.

Serves about 4 to 6.

Teriyaki Base:

"Use this base as a great glaze for grilled fish and meat. Simply brush on right before flipping and again right before removing from grill. It is also a great ingredient in sauces and salads."

$1/2$ cup **soy sauce**
1 tsp. **ginger, grated**
1 tsp. **green onion, chopped**
1 tsp. **garlic, chopped**
$1/2$ cup **brown sugar**

Combine soy sauce, ginger, onion and garlic in a small saucepan. Bring to a simmer over low heat. Just as it starts to simmer, stir in sugar until dissolved. Remove from heat, and chill.

Yields 1 cup.

SMOKED SALMON STRATA

Mary Ellen Summer
The Summer Inn Bed & Breakfast
Haines, AK

1 1/2 cups **bread pieces**
1 cup **smoked salmon, chopped**
2 cups **cheddar cheese, shredded**
2 cups **milk**
6 **eggs**
1/4 tsp. **dry mustard**
1/4 tsp. **cayenne pepper**
1/4 tsp. **paprika**
1/4 tsp. **pepper**
parsley for garnish

Arrange bread pieces in bottom of a greased 9" square pan. Layer smoked salmon and cheese over bread. Cover and refrigerate overnight.

In a medium bowl, beat milk, eggs and spices. Pour over refrigerated layers. Top with parsley. Bake at 375°F for 40 to 45 minutes.

Serves 6.

Contributors

A High Rigg Retreat B&B
#3 5119 RR 255
Spruce Grove, AB T7Y 1A8

A-1 Yankovich Inn B&B
2268 Yankovich Road
Fairbanks, AK 99709

Alaska Dancing Eagles B&B
   and Cabin Rentals
P.O. Box 264
Seldovia, AK 99663

Alaska Inn Between
   B&B and Cabins
P.O. Box 1209
Kasilof, AK 99610

Alaska Ocean View
   Bed & Breakfast Inn
1101 Edgecumbe Drive
Sitka, AK 99835

Alaska Wildland Adventures
P.O. Box 389
Girdwood, AK 99587

Arctic Circle Hot Springs
P.O. Box 30069
Central, AK 99730

Bear's Den Bed & Breakfast
P.O. Box 167
Seward, AK 99664

Beaver Point Lodge
P.O. Box 72648
Fairbanks, AK 99707

Billie's Backpackers Hostel
2895 Mack Blvd.
Fairbanks, AK 99709

Camp Denali/North Face Lodge
P.O. Box 67
Denali Park, AK 99755

Chena Hot Springs Resort
P.O. Box 58740
Fairbanks, AK 99511

Clam Gulch Lodge
P.O. Box 499
Clam Gulch, AK 99568

Cranberry Point Cabins and
   Bed and Breakfast
P.O. Box 20091
Whitehorse, YT Y1A 7A2

Coal River Lodge & RV
9515-95 Avenue
Fort St. John, BC V1J 1H7

Cow Bay Café
205 Cow Bay Road
Prince Rupert, BC V8J 1A2

EJ's Roost B&B
Box 1875
Grande Cache, AB P0E 0Y0

Fairbanks Bed and Breakfast
902 Kellum Street
Fairbanks, AK 99701

Girdwood Guest House
P.O. Box 67
Girdwood, AK 99587

Glacier Bay Country Inn
P.O. Box 5
Gustavus, AK 99826

Gracious House Lodge
P.O. Box 88
Cantwell, AK 99729

Grande Denali Lodge/
  Denali Bluffs Hotel
P.O. Box 72460
Fairbanks, AK 99707

Grand View Café &
  RV Campground
HC 03, Box 8484
Palmer, AK 99645

Gwin's Lodge & Restaurant
14865 Sterling Highway
Cooper Landing, AK 99572

Harley's Old Thyme Café
7559 Old Seward Highway
Anchorage, AK 99518

Hell's Gate Airtram, Inc./
  Salmon House Restaurant
Box 129
Hope, BC V0X 1L0

Kathy's Korner Bed & Breakfast
P.O. Box 42
Hyder, AK 99923

Kenai River Drifter's Lodge
P.O. Box 746
Cooper Landing, AK 99572

Kenai Riverfront B&B/RV Park
36193 Douglas Drive
Soldotna, AK 99669

Kennicott Glacier Lodge
P.O. Box 103940
Anchorage, AK 99510

Kidd's B&B
1524-113 Avenue
Dawson Creek, BC V1G 2Z5

Kincaid Grill
6700 Jewel Lake Road
Anchorage, AK 99502

Klondike Kate's
Box 417
Dawson City, YT Y0B 1L0

Kluane Bed & Breakfast
Box 5459
Haines Junction, YT Y0B 1L0

Lakeside Resort
RR 1, Site 21, Comp. 20
Vanderhoof, BC V01 3A0

Land's End Resort
4786 Homer Spit Road
Homer, AK 99603

Longmere Lake Lodge B&B
P.O. Box 1707
Soldotna, AK 99669

Mae's Kitchen
P.O. Box 35
Pink Mountain, BC V0C 2B0

Majestic Valley Wilderness Lodge
HC 03 Box 8514
Palmer, AK 99645

Mary's McKinley View Lodge
P.O. Box 13314
Trapper Creek, AK 99683

McKinley Foothills
  B&B and Cabins
P.O. Box 13089
Trapper Creek, AK 99683

Mentasta Lodge
HC 01 Box 585
Gakona, AK 99586

Midnight Sun Bed & Breakfast
6188 6th Avenue
Whitehorse, YT Y1A 1N8

Millennium Hotel
4800 Spenard Road
Anchorage, AK 99517

Mom's Sourdough Bakery
Box 21036
Whitehorse, YT Y1A 6P6

Mr. Whitekeys'
Fly by Night Club
3300 Spenard Road
Anchorage, AK 99517

Mykel's Restaurant
35041 Kenai Spur Highway
Soldotna, AK 99669

Nabesna House B&B
P.O. Box 970
Slana, AK 99586

Overlander Mountain Lodge
Box 6118
Hinton, AB T7V 1Z6

Overlook Bar & Grill at
Denali Crow's Nest Log Cabins
P.O. Box 70
Denali Park, AK 99755

Schwabenhof, Inc.
P.O. Box 876482
Wasilla, AK 99687

7 Gables Inn & Suites
P.O. Box 80488
Fairbanks, AK 99708

Seven Glaciers Restaurant/
Alyeska Resort
P.O. Box 249
Girdwood, AK 99587

Sheep Mountain Lodge
HC 03 Box 8490
Palmer, AK 99645

Skyline Bed and Breakfast
63540 Skyline Drive
Homer, AK 99603

Sourdough Roadhouse
P.O. Box 358
Gakona, AK 99586

Spruce Acre Cabins
910 Sterling Highway
Homer, AK 99503

Summit Lake Lodge
51826 Seward Highway
Moose Pass, AK 99631

Sunrise Inn
P.O. Box 832
Cooper Landing, AK 99572

Talkeetna Alaskan Lodge
P.O. Box 727
Talkeetna, AK 99676

Talkeetna Roadhouse
P.O. Box 604
Talkeetna, AK 99676

The Bake Shop
P.O. Box 115
Girdwood, AK 99587

The Lakehouse
P.O. Box 770
Valdez, AK 99686

The Perch
P.O. Box 53
Denali Park, AK 99755

The Saltry
Kachemak Bay
9 W. Ismilof
Halibut Cove, AK 99603

The Shepherd's Inn Ltd.
Box 6425
Fort St. John, BC V1J 4H8

The Summer Inn Bed & Breakfast
117 Second Avenue
P.O. Box 1198
Haines, AK 99827

Tundra Rose Bed & Breakfast
HC 03 Box 8484
Palmer, AK 99645

Turnagain House
HC Box 8654
Indian, AK 99540

Tutka Bay Wilderness Lodge
P.O. Box 960
Homer, AK 99603

Two Rivers Lodge
4968 Chena Hot Springs Road
Fairbanks, AK 99712

Varly's Swiftwater Seafood Café
P.O. Box 681
Whittier, AK 99693

Walkabout Town
  Bed & Breakfast
1610 E Street
Anchorage, AK 99501

Wildflour Coffee Shop
P.O. Box 132
Hyder, AK 99923

Index

Cakes

Candy

Cereals

Chicken (see Poultry)

Clams (see also Seafood)

Cookies

Crab (see also Seafood)

Desserts (see also Cakes, Cookies & Pies)

Egg Dishes

Game Meats

Halibut

Jams, Jellies & Preserves

Meat (see also Beef, Game Meats, Pork, Poultry)

Muffins

Pancakes

Pasta

Pies

Pork

Potatoes

Poultry

Quiches

Rhubarb

Salads & Salad Dressings

Salmon

Sauces, Spreads & Syrups

Seafood (see also Clams, Crab, Halibut & Salmon)

Soups

Sourdough

Vegetables